Stop Smoking

FOR

DUMMIES®

Stop Smoking

FOR

DUMMIES®

by Sally Lewis and David Brizer

John Wiley & Sons, Ltd

Stop Smoking For Dummies®

Published by
John Wiley & Sons, Ltd
The Atrium
Southern Gate
Chichester
West Sussex
PO19 8SQ
England

E-mail (for orders and customer service enquires): cs-books@wiley.co.uk

Visit our Home Page on www.wiley.com

For general information on our other products and services, please contact our Customer Care Department within the U.S. at 800-762-2974, outside the U.S. at 317-572-3993, or fax 317-572-4002.

For technical support, please visit www.wiley.com/techsupport.

Wiley also publishes its books in a variety of electronic formats. Some content that appears in print may not be available in electronic books.

British Library Cataloguing in Publication Data: A catalogue record for this book is available from the British Library

ISBN: 978-0-470-99456-6

Printed and bound in Great Britain by Page Bros

10 9 8 7 6 5 4 3 2 1

About the Authors

Sally Lewis is a qualified health and fitness instructor and has been involved in the field of health, well-being, and fitness for more years than she cares to remember. She has participated in numerous health projects and taught on fitness, diet and health courses, workshops, and seminars. A health consultant to many private organisations and health authorities in the UK, she thrives on supporting, encouraging, and enabling individuals to achieve their personal health and fitness goals. She has appeared as a health and lifestyle consultant on television and radio, and has written several health, diet, and fitness books. Sally is also well known for her health features in several national magazines. When not lecturing, writing, or instructing, Sally can be found running in the woods with her dog and husband in the beautiful New Forest where they live.

David Brizer, MD, chairman of psychiatry at Norwalk Hospital in Norwalk, Connecticut, has written half a dozen books on addiction, healthcare, and psychiatry. Dr Brizer received his MD degree from the Albert Einstein College of Medicine and his psychiatry training at the Payne Whitney Clinic in New York. He has been treating people with addictive disorders for two decades. Dr Brizer also serves as medical editor of *Mental Health News* and publishes numerous articles, papers, and chapters in the field.

Dedication

This book is dedicated to every person who wants something better in life – to every hero who has or will quit smoking.

Authors' Acknowledgements

From Sally: My first thanks must be to my family who so graciously realised that my deadline coincided with Christmas and the New Year – I promise to get the wrapping done before 1 a.m. Christmas Day next year! To Mark who has such patience and remains calm no matter what I throw at him. What would I do without you? To my sons, Alex and Harrison who both know just how I feel about the damage smoking does to both the body and soul.

To Mum and Dad, for being there, picking up the dog and the boys when necessary and making the tea. To Wejdan and her team at Wiley and to James, my agent, who took over the reins half way through the publication.

To all my clients, without whom I would not make a living or be able to write about you – all nice things of course! Well done to all of you for achieving your goals and improving your health and well-being. Your success is my success – thank you. I look forward to the next set of challenges you present me with.

From David: The following people have inspired me by their example, their support, and their wisdom:

Carol Bauer
George Bauer
Alex Brizer
Max Brizer
Ricardo Castaneda, MD
Helen During
Max Ernst
Marc Estrin
Jonathan Fine, MD
Claudia Fletcher
Peter Green
Margaret Haggerty, APRN
Joris-Karl Huysmans
Alfred Jarry
Amy Levin

Barbara McCormick
Harry de Meo, MD
Harry Mathews
Solomon Moses
Paul Nurick
David Osborne
Whitney Pastorek
Phil & Frank
Professor Tammy
Robert Ready
Maura Romaine
Raymond Roussel
Gustav Vintas
Marianne Williamson
Stephen Winter, MD

Publisher's Acknowledgements

We're proud of this book; please send us your comments through our Dummies online registration form located at www.dummies.com/register/.

Some of the people who helped bring this book to market include the following:

Acquisitions, Editorial, and Media Development

Project Editor: Simon Bell

Content Editor: Nicole Burnett

Acquisitions Editor: Wejdan Ismail

Developer: Kelly Ewing

Copy Editor: Martin Key

Proofreader: Mary White

Technical Editor: Dr Sarah Brewer

Publisher: Jason Dunne

Executive Editor:
Samantha Spickernell

Executive Project Editor:
Daniel Mersey

Cover Photos:
Oote Boe Photography 3 / Alamy

Cartoons: Ed McLachlan

Composition Services

Project Coordinator: Erin Smith

Layout and Graphics: Stacie Brooks, Reuben W. Davis, Joyce Haughey, Melissa K. Jester, Stephanie D. Jumper

Special Art:

Proofreaders: Laura Albert, Melanie Hoffman

Indexer: Cheryl Duksta

Contents at a Glance

Introduction 1

Part I: Taking Stock: Your Decision to Stop 7

Chapter 1: Calling It Quits 9
Chapter 2: Working Out Why You Smoke 23
Chapter 3: Evaluating the Health Risks of Smoking 37

Part II: Packing It In 51

Chapter 4: Just Stopping...53
Chapter 5: Using Nicotine Replacement Therapies 67
Chapter 6: Tapping in to the Power of the Mind 83
Chapter 7: Staying Smoke Free 95

Part III: Looking at Special Groups 115

Chapter 8: Smoking, Depression, and Weight Gain 117
Chapter 9: Smoking, Fertility, and Pregnancy 131

Part IV: The Part of Tens 141

Chapter 10: Ten Signs That You're Ready to Stop.............................143
Chapter 11: Ten Great Smoking Substitutes......................................151
Chapter 12: Ten Sources of Support 159

Index 167

Table of Contents

Introduction *1*

   About This Book..1
   Conventions Used in This Book 2
   Foolish Assumptions 2
   How This Book Is Organised...3
      Part I: Taking Stock: Your Decision to Stop...............3
      Part II: Packing It In..4
      Part III: Looking at Special Groups 4
      Part IV: The Part of Tens...5
   Icons Used in This Book...5
   Where to Go from Here...5

Part 1: Taking Stock: Your Decision to Stop *7*

   Chapter 1: Calling It Quits **9**

      Making the Decision..9
      Getting a Fresh Start 11
      Coming to Terms with Your Addiction 13
      Knowing When You're Ready to Stop 16
      Finding Quitting Aids 17
         Prescription and over-the-counter NRTs.................17
         Alternative quitting methods 19

   Chapter 2: Working Out Why You Smoke **23**

      Looking at the Benefits and Risks of Smoking....................24
      Understanding What Addiction Is...26
      Recognising Why You Started...27

Understanding Why You Smoke Now 28
    It's an addiction 29
    Smoking meets your emotional needs......................30
    You use smoking to control your weight.................31
    You use smoking to control stress 32
Teenagers: Smoking to Be Cool 33
Understanding the Effects of Nicotine on Your Brain 34

**Chapter 3: Evaluating the Health Risks of
    Smoking. 37**

Damaging the Respiratory System..38
Smoking Out the Health Risks of Tobacco..........................40
    Smoke gets in your eyes (and mouth and
        heart and lungs) 40
    Cigarettes and cancer: A match made
        in heaven 43
    Nicotine puts your body on high alert....................44
    Mental effects..47
    Smoker's cough..48
Quitting While You're Ahead 48

Part II: Packing It In 51

Chapter 4: Just Stopping 53

Planning a Date..53
Letting Go 54
Doing Without: The Cold-Turkey Method 56
Cutting Back Gradually..59
Giving It Up and Getting Rewards?......................................59
Dealing with the Changes..60
Evaluating What Went Wrong 61

**Chapter 5: Using Nicotine Replacement
    Therapies 67**

Exploring Nicotine Replacement Therapies 68
Using NRTs Safely...69

Trying Over-the-Counter NRTs 70
   Using the nicotine patch...71
   Chewing cravings away with nicotine gum 73
   Giving nicotine lozenges a try....................................75
   Succumbing to a microbtab 76
Talking It Over with Your Doc: Prescription-Only
   Options...76
   Considering nicotine inhalers 77
   Using nicotine nasal spray 78
   Trying out anti-craving medication.........................78
Combining Quitting Aids 80

Chapter 6: Tapping in to the Power of the Mind 83

Using Your Mind to Help You Stop Smoking......................84
Figuring Out What Hypnosis Is All About 85
Contemplating Meditation 86
   So what exactly is meditation? 87
   Appreciating and controlling your breathing 88
Changing the Way You Think...89
Maximising Your Motivation...90
Exorcising Nicotine with Exercise.......................................91
Trying Acupuncture...93

Chapter 7: Staying Smoke Free 95

Planning a Strategy for Success 95
Finding a Quitting Buddy 99
Sticking with Stopping..99
   Assessing your relapse risk....................................100
   Watching out for common relapse triggers...........101
   Staying on track 102
Handling Relapses...106
   Staying focused 108
   Reframing relapse: A day without nicotine
      is a successful day!...109
Handling Second-Hand Smoke When You're a Quitter 111
Developing Cognitive Skills for Success............................112

Part III: Looking at Special Groups 115

Chapter 8: Smoking, Depression, and Weight Gain 117

What Is Depression? 118
Alleviating Anxiety 119
    The principle of drug karma 121
    Cognitive behavioural therapy 123
The Truth about Quitting Smoking and Weight Gain.......124
    Staying away from fattening quick-fix foods 126
    Doing your part by exercising regularly................127
    Finding food substitutes for nicotine.....................128

Chapter 9: Smoking, Fertility, and Pregnancy 131

Smoking and Fertility...132
    Risks to the foetus...133
    Smoking-related complications................................134
Stopping Smoking During Pregnancy 136
Smoking and Breast Feeding..137
The Long-Term Effects of Maternal Smoking....................138

Part IV: The Part of Tens 141

Chapter 10: Ten Signs That You're Ready to Stop 143

You're Developing a Smoker's Cough 143
Your Wallet Feels the Crunch..144
You're Willing to Walk a Mile for a Cigarette....................144
You Feel Like a Social Misfit...145
You're Unable to _____ (Fill in the Blank)
    without a Smoke..145

You Feel Guilty 146
You Smoke More and Enjoy It Less 147
You React to Negative Comments 147
You Miss Your Senses of Smell and Taste 148
You Want a Healthier Future 148

Chapter 11: Ten Great Smoking Substitutes 151

Working Out 152
Having More Time 152
Drinking Lots of Fluids...153
Meditating 153
Reaping the Power of Positive Thinking 154
Using Nicotine Replacement Therapies 154
Getting Five a Day 155
Visualising Health..155
Changing Your Routine...156
Getting a Piggy Bank 157

Chapter 12: Ten Sources of Support 159

Buy This Book for You and Your Smoking Friends 159
Use the Internet..160
Take Advantage of Group Support.....................................160
Talk to Your Family and Friends...161
Call a Counsellor 161
Volunteer 162
Join a Health Club 162
Hire a Personal Trainer 164
Make the Smoking Laws Work for You...............................164
Write a Blog..165

Index *167*

Introduction

● ●

*L*ong before medical science came up with sophisti-
cated explanations for addiction, people were using
tobacco. In the 20th century, cigarette smoking in
Western nations became pandemic. Reaching for a cigarette after a meal, at the office, in the theatre, or on a
plane became as normal as having a cup of tea. However,
a harsher light has now been shed on smoking, prompt-
ing the introduction of new smoking laws in the UK and
parts of Europe to protect people from the damaging
effects of cigarette smoke.

The decision to stop smoking is far from a casual one.
Stopping smoking involves your complete commitment. It
must become your (not your spouse's or your best friend's)
number-one priority. Mustering all the support you can get,
you need to decide to turn up the flame of your survival
instinct, your belief in a healthy future, and your willpower
and believe that you can, and will, quit.

Throughout this book, we share strategies, tools, and
action plans to help make your decision to stop effective
and permanent.

About This Book

You don't need to know much about medicine or chemistry to find this book useful. *Stop Smoking For Dummies*
covers a lot of ground, but it does so in a friendly, accessible, and non-academic way. The last thing you need at

this great milestone in your life is an unsympathetic voice from an ivory tower. At the same time, we give you the latest, most useful, and most accurate health-related information available today.

This book does not propose any particular route to follow. You get to explore the many options described in this book and choose the ones that work for you. Millions of people have stopped smoking by using many different methods – no single formula for success exists.

Conventions Used in This Book

Like all the books in the *For Dummies* series, *Stop Smoking For Dummies* is highly structured. You can skip to any section that appeals to you and dive into the chapters and sections at will – you don't need to read in sequence. Find what interests you and start at that topic.

You'll also see little grey boxes, known as *sidebars,* throughout the book. These sidebars complement the main text and contain interesting extra information, but if you're short on time or aren't interested, you can skip over them without missing any critical points.

Foolish Assumptions

If you're stopping smoking for the first time, this book is for you. If you've tried to stop in the past, this book is for you. And if you aren't a smoker yourself but you care deeply about someone who is, this book is also for you.

As we wrote this book, we made the following assumptions:

- ✒ You'll take this book's suggestions within the larger context of your personal health. If you have one or more medical conditions, you'll discuss with your doctor the pros and cons of nicotine-replacement therapies or other interventions mentioned in this book.

- ✒ You don't just live for the moment. You believe in and plan for the future and care about your health and wellbeing.

You should always consult your doctor before you make any lifestyle changes that involve your health.

How This Book Is Organised

This book is organised into four parts, each of which covers a major area of stopping smoking. Each part is then divided into chapters that give you the focus you need to stop for good. The following sections summarise each part.

Part 1: Taking Stock: Your Decision to Stop

Your decision to stop smoking is great! This milestone deserves as much attention as you can muster. This part of the book helps you analyse where you're coming from: why you started smoking in the first place, and why you continue to smoke today. It also helps you define where you want to go.

You also discover a great deal of information about nicotine addiction and why you may be using nicotine to control weight and stress. You find out why teenagers smoke and what effects you have on them if you continue to smoke, as well as the risks that you are posing to your health every time you light up.

As you evaluate the downsides of smoking, your motivation to cast smoking aside increases.

Part II: Packing It In

The best quitter is usually an informed quitter. In this part, you arm yourself with the information you need to stop permanently, and discover the many alternatives to smoking, such as the nicotine patch and nicotine gum. You also find out about other alternative methods that smokers often try in an effort to rid themselves of their habit, such as meditation, hypnosis, and other positive mind-changing techniques.

In addition, Part II helps you create a specific and detailed plan to stop smoking. It also provides tips on how to remain a non-smoker, especially when you're dealing with a relapse.

Part III: Looking at Special Groups

You don't have to belong to any particular group or demographic to get mileage out of this part. These chapters cover smoking's effect on fertility, for both men and women, and talk about stopping smoking during pregnancy. This part also contains a chapter about the effects of depression and how nicotine actually increases your chances of becoming depressed.

Part IV: The Part of Tens

The Part of Tens is an essential part of every *For Dummies* book. In this part, you find quick and dirty information on how to know you're ready to quit, what to substitute for your smoking habit, and where you can go to find support.

Icons Used in This Book

Throughout this book, *icons* help guide you on your cessation voyage. The icons are strategically placed to reinforce the most important information in the book. Here's what the icons mean:

This icon highlights better, faster, and easier ways to approach various aspects of stopping smoking.

This icon draws your attention to areas of particular caution as well as traps and triggers that often cause quitters to relapse or keep smokers from attempting to stop in the first place.

This icon points to words of wisdom that are worth remembering over the long haul. If you want a quick summary of the essential information in this book, just read the text next to this icon.

Where to Go from Here

Where you go from here depends on where you are in your journey to stop smoking. The information in this book is intended to be as accessible and immediate as possible. When you want to find out about a particular topic, feel free to go to the pertinent chapter or section. The table of contents at the front of the book and the index at the back can help you find your way.

Good luck on your journey to better health and wellbeing and a new nicotine-free you.

Part I
Taking Stock: Your Decision to Stop

'I realise you gave up smoking a month ago, Miss Snagthorpe, but it does take time to clear your system.'

In this part . . .

Smoking is an addiction, a compulsion, and an appetite that takes on a life of its own. Deciding to stop smoking is a major life step that requires understanding, knowledge, and courage. Knowing the facts about the consequences of smoking on your health both physically and mentally, the realities of addiction, and the attraction of nicotine to teenagers helps you stand by your decision to stop. This part's puff-by-puff guide to understanding why you smoke, and the impact that smoking has on you and those around you, clears the air. The more information you have, the better equipped you are to succeed.

Chapter 1

Calling It Quits

∙ ∙

In This Chapter

▶ Getting in the right frame of mind

▶ Looking forward to life after stopping

▶ Admitting that you're addicted to cigarettes

▶ Knowing when you're ready to stop

▶ Tooling up for success

▶ Finding the support you need to make quitting last

∙ ∙

*S*topping smoking is a major commitment and an enormously positive life step. If you're like most smokers, you've tried to stop before. You probably appreciate the difficulty and some of the complexities involved in kicking the habit. This chapter discusses the major issues involved in stopping smoking.

Making the Decision

Ever want to call it quits? Ever feel like you've just had enough (cigarettes, I mean)? If so, welcome to the crowd. Millions of people have been through this experience, and millions of people have succeeded at stopping smoking. This book guides you through the process and is a friend, a tool, a source of information, and a weapon.

Stopping smoking is one of the best and most important things you can do for yourself.

The best way to stop smoking is to do it comprehensively. This book arms and fortifies you not only with the facts, but also with self-knowledge and commitment on an intellectual, emotional, and perhaps even spiritual level.

Why do you want to stop smoking?

✔ Maybe you think you need to for your health, although you would prefer to smoke forever. (If there was a way to make cigarettes harmless, it would have been done. Tobacco companies have spent millions on research, and cigarettes are as deadly today as they've always been.)

✔ Maybe you've been asked or told by friends and family that you really should stop smoking. There's that nagging cough and that tell-tale odour on your clothes, in your house, and in your car. Your kids, if you have kids, can't be happy about your habit – unless they smoke too.

✔ Or maybe it's the very idea of being addicted to something. Have you ever had the experience of running out of the house in the middle of the night to find a convenience store that can service your need?

When you think about it, smoking is a gruesome process. The ingredients of tobacco are no better than what comes pouring out of the chimneys of factories or a car's exhaust pipe. Along with nicotine, the fumes contain carbon monoxide, tar, and literally thousands of other chemicals, dozens of which are known to harm the body.

The most important step in the process of stopping smoking is to make the decision to stop.

Getting a Fresh Start

Stopping smoking is going to be tough, and yes, you'll face challenges along the way, but you can do it. You can recreate yourself without cigarettes. Chapter 4 discusses in detail the ways you can go about stopping smoking. Choosing a single method or combining the many options you have to stop is down to your own choice. Remember, there are many agencies to support you through this time.

When you decide to stop is a great time to take a detailed, point-by-point inventory of what you want your life to be like after you stop smoking.

To create this inventory, write down all the steps and actions you need to take to turn yourself into the person you want to be once you have given up smoking. Table 1-1 helps you identify exactly what steps you need to take to accomplish your goals.

Table 1-1 Who Will I Be After Stopping? Action Plan

Category	*Steps I Need to Take to Achieve My Goals*
Career goals	
Educational goals	
Non-work/school-related activities	
Financial goals	

continued

Table 1-1 c*ontinued*

Category	Steps I Need to Take to Achieve My Goals
Emotional goals	
Spiritual goals	
Other goals	
Goals for the coming month	
Goals for the coming year	
Goals for the long term	

Writing down your goals gives you some strong reasons to believe that there is life after cigarettes. And the life you have after cigarettes, just like the life you've had while smoking, is to a large extent shaped by the decisions you make.

Stopping smoking is not a simple act. Because smoking has played so many pivotal roles in your life, stopping is a highly complex process. When you give up such an important part of your life, you need to replace it with something just as compelling and powerful. See Chapter 7 to find out how to stay smoke-free, especially when you run into temptation around the corner.

The smoking laws apply to you at work and at play.

The smoking laws and how they affect you

Since 1 July 2007, virtually all enclosed public places and workplaces in the UK have become smoke-free zones. In fact, if you want a cigarette, you have to go outside.

Bars, clubs, cafes, shops, offices, and factories are all smoke-free areas, and employers no longer have to provide indoor smoking areas for smokers. Smoking on public transport, such as buses, trains, and taxis, is also illegal, and if you have a work vehicle, don't think you can have a crafty puff in that either! Smoking in these places is now against the law, and if you do smoke in them then you are likely to be fined.

Look on the bright side: It seems everyone is trying to help you to give up smoking. In fact, the reason for the new laws is the health damage that second-hand smoke causes.

So if you can't smoke at work or out and about socially, doesn't it tell you something? Smoking really is dangerous, damaging, and life-threatening. Do you need any more reasons to stop?

Coming to Terms with Your Addiction

You may feel that you can handle smoking and that it isn't a problem for you. So how do you know when you need to stop?

Why did you buy this book? You may know people who have been harmed by smoking and have become ill, either acutely or chronically. Friends or relatives may have suggested or hinted that it may be a good idea for you to cut back on cigarettes or to stop altogether. (Those friends or relatives may even have given you this book.) Do you worry about the effects of smoking on your health, your appearance, and your wallet? Do you ever resent having to make allowances, find excuses, and look for opportunities to get outside to find a private spot to light up?

Your decision to stop smoking is based on personal motivations.

Tobacco toxicity comes in many forms. Tobacco and the chemicals and additives it contains are physically harmful, have powerful effects on behaviour and the nervous system, and have a widespread negative impact on public health as well.

Ask yourself whether smoking is making problems for you. Once you have a crystal-clear understanding of the actual and potential damage that smoking causes, you will feel less doubtful and more committed than ever to stopping smoking. If you are pregnant, you have an extra reason to stop smoking. (Chapter 9 discusses the effects of nicotine on the foetus and may give you the ammunition you need to help stop.)

Whatever your reason to stop, top it up by understanding as much as possible about the intermediate and long-term consequences of smoking. You'll get to a point where justifying more smoking is no longer possible.

You need to come to terms with your level of smoking in order to become ready to stop. (See the next section for help on knowing when you're ready to stop.) Maybe you need to understand that you are addicted to nicotine.

Chapter 2 discusses the reasons why you smoke; understanding your motivation can help you in your quest to quit.

If you think that smoking isn't a problem for you, you're unlikely to dedicate your heart and soul to stopping. On the other hand, if you take an honest self-inventory of your commitment to smoking, you may want to stop . . . yesterday!

One sure sign that you're really hooked is the presence of nicotine withdrawal symptoms. These highly unpleasant sensations arise within one or two hours of your last cigarette and include:

- ✔ Irritability
- ✔ Fatigue
- ✔ Mood swings
- ✔ Insomnia (inability to sleep) or hypersomnia (too much sleep)
- ✔ Trouble concentrating
- ✔ Headaches
- ✔ Increased appetite
- ✔ Anxiety
- ✔ Depression
- ✔ Shifting energy levels

These withdrawal symptoms naturally lead to cravings for a cigarette.

As you think about stopping, consider how powerful a hold nicotine has on you. Anything that can cause withdrawal symptoms like these is powerful and ultimately toxic. Do you really want to be a slave to something so terrible for you? (To understand the health implications of nicotine, see Chapter 3.)

As you come to understand the impact that smoking has on your life, you may feel slightly overwhelmed. Fortunately, you get lots of chances in life, including the chance to stop smoking and recapture part or all of your physical health.

Knowing When You're Ready to Stop

You're ready to stop smoking when:

- ✔ You've decided that stopping smoking is the most important goal in your life.

- ✔ You accept the fact that in order to get ahead and get more of the things you want, such as health, wellbeing, and self-respect, you have to make sacrifices.

- ✔ You feel a sense of responsibility, not only towards yourself, but towards your family, your friends, and even your pets.

You can look at this move in many ways. Hopefully you see your decision to stop as positive, life-affirming, and absolutely necessary. Stopping smoking feels like deprivation, like a wicked, deep loss. There's no getting around it: It *is* a loss. But it's a loss that brings you a great deal of gain at the same time.

Finding Quitting Aids

You must be prepared to face both the physical and psychological manifestations of nicotine withdrawal. When you smoke, the amount of nicotine in your blood rises. The nicotine in the blood passes through every part of the body. In the brain, nicotine triggers different receptors, and these receptors get used to a customary level of nicotine in your blood. When that level drops, such as after a night's sleep, your brain wants more nicotine, *now.*

Stopping smoking is war. The more weapons you have to fight with, the better your chances of stopping for good. That's why a combination of strategies works best for many people (see Chapter 5). Nicotine replacement therapies (NRTs) are a reasonable way to substitute plain old nicotine for smoking, which comes with a host of other poisons that your body doesn't need. NRTs are designed to wean you off tobacco without withdrawal symptoms.

Smoking-cessation programmes take many forms. Use the tools that are available to help you win the war. Nicotine is a serious and deadly opponent.

Prescription and over-the-counter NRTs

Most NRTs are available over the counter, but how do you know what will work best for you? Your doctor or a qualified cessation counsellor can help you find the optimal therapy for your personal situation.

Chewing gum may be the answer if you need some kind of substitute oral gratification. Or maybe the convenience of the patch makes it the optimal NRT for you. Are you looking for rapidity of action? Then nicotine nasal spray may be the solution. Do you miss the feel of a cigarette in your hand? Consider using a nicotine inhaler.

The following list provides some basic information about NRTs. (See Chapter 5 for details about these quitting aids.)

✔ **Nicotine patch:** The patch, available both over the counter and by prescription, delivers nicotine to your system through your skin. You use patches of decreasing strength until your body no longer craves nicotine.

✔ **Nicotine gum:** This over-the-counter product works similarly to the patch. The gum delivers nicotine to your body, and you wean yourself off by chewing less and less.

✔ **Nicotine nasal spray:** You inhale this spray through your nose, delivering nicotine to your system quickly. It provides almost instantaneous relief of cravings and other nicotine withdrawal symptoms. It's considered very effective for heavy smokers.

✔ **Nicotine inhalers:** This method delivers a fine mist containing nicotine to the lining of the mouth, giving the user more of an oral feel, which many smokers miss when they try to stop.

✔ **Nicotine lozenges:** Nicotine lozenges are like throat lozenges, except that instead of soothing a sore throat, they reduce nicotine cravings by supplying the body with nicotine.

Zyban (chemical name bupropion) is an antidepressant that's been found to reduce nicotine cravings and other withdrawal symptoms. It can be used alone or in combination with one of the other NRTs. Only a doctor can prescribe it. Combining Zyban and an NRT may be even more effective than either approach by itself.

Alternative quitting methods

NRTs and/or Zyban alone may not be enough support for you. A wide variety of alternative quitting methods are available, and you can use them to complement rather than substitute for NRTs:

- ✔ **Champix:** A non-nicotine therapy available only on prescription. It is taken 8–14 days before you actually stop smoking and then afterwards for approximately 12 weeks. Motivational support is offered to every patient who is prescribed Champix.

  Champix has the generic name varenicline. The drug works by reducing withdrawal symptoms, producing nicotine-like effects by binding to receptors in the brain. It also reduces the satisfaction smokers receive from a cigarette if they smoke while using this drug.

- ✔ **Quitlines:** Telephone counsellors are available to help you. Call the NHS Smoking Helpline on 0800 169 0169 or Quitline on 0800 002 200.

- ✔ **Support groups:** Evidence shows that having a network of friends and family to provide emotional support as you stop smoking increases your likelihood of quitting permanently. (Turn to Chapter 12 for unusual forms of support that you may find useful.)

✔ **Quit-smoking programmes:** The NHS's Together Programme offers information packs and text message, e-mail, and telephone support. You can do it all from the comfort of your home. Don't forget it's all free too! QUIT offers specialist clinics and support groups in your area – phone 0800 002 200 to find out where and for further details, or email `info@quit.org.uk`.

You can get information on these support groups from your GP, pharmacy, local health centre or local library.

✔ **Acupuncture and hypnotherapy:** Both of these alternative methods have been found to be very successful for a number of people stopping smoking. Make sure you find a qualified practitioner. The following organisations can provide lists of qualified practitioners.

- British Acupuncture Council (BAcC), 63 Jeddo Road, London W12 9HQ; tel 020 8735 0400, Web site `www.acupuncture.org.uk`.

- The British Complementary Medicine Association, PO Box 5122, Bournemouth BH8 0WG; tel 0845 345 5977, Web site `www.bcma.co.uk`.

- The Institute For Complementary Medicine, ICM Unit 25, Tavern Quay Business Centre, Sweden Gate, London SE16 7TX; tel 020 7231 5855, Web site `www.i-c-m.org.uk`.

Chapter 6, Tapping in to the Power of the Mind, has further details on using mind techniques to help you stop smoking.

The more strategies and tactics you use, the more likely you are to succeed at stopping. Do whatever it takes to stop and stay that way!

Chapter 2

Working Out Why You Smoke

In This Chapter

▶ Weighing the risks of smoking against the benefits

▶ Thinking about the addictive nature of nicotine

▶ Looking at why you started smoking in the first place

▶ Being honest with yourself about why you smoke now

▶ Considering why teenagers are attracted to nicotine

▶ Finding out what nicotine does to your brain

*W*hy would anyone *choose* to smoke? Beyond a certain point, of course, you really stop choosing. In fact, many smokers want to stop but can't because of their addiction to nicotine. Nicotine is one of the most fiercely addictive substances on earth. This fact has been borne out in numerous studies of both laboratory animals and humans. Stopping smoking is tough.

Addiction to tobacco and nicotine has both physical and psychological components. Laboratory experiments have demonstrated that among drugs of abuse, such as heroin and cocaine, nicotine is way up there on the habit-forming scale. Like many other behaviours, addiction has many factors. Whether you get hooked on cigarettes has a lot to do with who you are, how you handle things, your family background, and the environment in which you place yourself.

They say that knowledge is power. Knowing more about why you smoke arms you for the leap into smoke-free freedom.

Looking at the Benefits and Risks of Smoking

Stopping smoking is one of the best and most important things you can do for yourself. You must arm and fortify yourself not only with the facts, but also with self-knowledge and with commitment on an intellectual, emotional, and perhaps even spiritual level.

Within 24 hours of stopping smoking, carbon monoxide is eliminated from your body, and your lungs start to clear out mucus and other smoking debris.

Think about why you want to stop. Perhaps you want to stop because all your friends have stopped, even though you'd prefer to keep on smoking. Take an in-depth look at the personal costs and benefits of smoking. Take a pen to paper and draw a line down the centre of the page. Label one column *Benefits of Smoking* and the other *Risks of Smoking,* as in Table 2-1. Then, in each column, fill in what you think are the benefits and risks of this habit.

Table 2-1 Charting the Benefits and Risks of Smoking

Benefits of Smoking	*Risks of Smoking*

Devote as much time as you need during an undistracted part of your day to completing this chart. Search your own memories and experiences as well as the experiences of others to come up with items for each list. The items that jump to mind first are likely to be those that are most immediate and contemporary for you. You can always add to your list later. Assign points to each of the items on your list, using the following scale: 1 means that the risk/benefit has little impact on your life, while 10 means that the item has enormous impact. Add up the columns and see what you come up with. Do the risks outweigh the benefits?

The tobacco–alcohol link

Numerous studies have linked the use of tobacco to other legal and illegal substances, in particular alcohol. People who drink to excess are also usually dependent upon nicotine. This combination is deadly, causing an increase in mortality rates for the individuals who use both substances, and it has an impact on public health and society in general.

The tobacco–alcohol link involves complex biological, social, and chemical aspects. Nicotine and alcohol stimulate neuroreceptors in the brain giving rise to pleasurable and reinforcing effects. Nicotine increases or stimulates the urge to drink, and vice versa. Physiologically, alcohol is metabolised more quickly if nicotine is present, so you need more alcohol for the desired result if you smoke.

Alcohol and smoking greatly increase your risk of mouth, pharyngeal, and oesophageal cancer.

Understanding What Addiction Is

The thing about addiction is you don't know you're hooked until it's too late. Nicotine is just as addictive as cocaine or heroin, and all smokers self–administer nicotine. According to the World Health Organization, addiction is defined as:

> *A state, psychic and sometimes also physical, resulting in the interaction between a living organism and a drug, characterised by behavioural and other responses that always include a compulsion to take the*

drug on a continuous or periodic basis in order to experience its psychic effects, and sometimes to avoid the discomfort of its absences.

Addiction is any behaviour that's repeated over and over despite negative consequences, and is elective; you choose to do it, initially at least, until you become addicted. Another term for addiction is dependence (as in chemical dependence).

Nicotine both stimulates and relaxes, and it is not just your mental and physical state, or the situation you find yourself in, that affects how you react to lighting up a cigarette, but the direct effect that nicotine has on your brain. Dopamine, a chemical in the brain associated with pleasure, is released each time you smoke, but you have to smoke more and more to get the same level of stimulation. Getting hooked is easy.

Each cigarette shortens your life by 11 minutes.

Recognising Why You Started

Why did you start smoking? The next time you're with one or more fellow smokers, consider asking this question. Imagine the variety of responses you'll get.

You may have started smoking because

- ✔ Your partner, spouse, or close friends did.
- ✔ Cigarettes were less expensive than food.
- ✔ You wanted to be defiant.
- ✔ You wanted to make a statement.
- ✔ Cigarettes helped you relax.

✔ You felt part of a group who smoked.

✔ You identified with a film star who smoked in a film.

✔ You smoked only when you were drinking and partying.

✔ You wanted to appear older than you really were.

Undoubtedly, you can add other reasons to this list. You may have thought that smoking was cool or that you were invincible, or you may have taken a philosophical stance that smoking was okay. Whatever your reason for picking up the smoking habit, that reason is definitely not the reason you have continued to smoke. Smoking is addictive, and the personal choice to smoke or not to smoke probably left the building long ago.

There are 12 million ex-smokers in the UK. If they can do it, so can you!

Understanding Why You Smoke Now

Regular smoking means that you are addicted to a drug – a chemical substance – which you take for its pleasurable effects. And whether you like it or not, nicotine is one of the most deadly, addictive drugs about – just think about lung cancer and emphysema, for starters. So powerful is this addiction that many smokers are reluctant to stop smoking even after having surgery for smoking-related illnesses and disease.

Smoking-related deaths are usually attributable to lung cancer, heart disease, or chronic pulmonary obstructive disease (COPD).

It's an addiction

Many people, including non-smokers, make light of tobacco addiction. It's as though an unspoken scale of addiction severity exists, with tobacco coming in somewhere on the less severe end of things. 'Bad' addictions include illegal drugs like crack and heroin.

Actually, nicotine is one of the most addictive substances known to exist. The reason you smoke in spite of your reluctance to do so is precisely because nicotine is so addictive.

Nicotine is both a stimulant and a sedative, and like any drug, it gives you a variety of different feelings.

Cut yourself a mental break. Don't give up on stopping just because it seems so difficult. Many others have been down this road, and you can succeed at stopping too.

Smoking is usually not hidden or covert. The habit is highly visible. But compared to other addictions, addiction to tobacco is more challenging to your life and more demanding of your time. Believe it or not, many users of opiates, heroin, and methadone continue for years and even decades without becoming ill. 'Maintenance' drinkers regularly consume alcohol over a lifetime, sometimes with less-drastic consequences than may follow from continued smoking. Granted, you may be able to think of friends or acquaintances who smoke without health consequences, but healthy long-term smokers are the exception. Think about the long-term smokers you know. A smoker's cough is not a sign of robust health!

Don't minimise the seriousness of smoking. Just because millions of people do it and it's legal, it doesn't reduce the gravity of the potential harm that smoking can cause.

Tobacco is not competing with any other drugs or substances for first prize among addictions. Still, if such a prize existed, tobacco might win the blue ribbon. What other addiction – including alcoholism and dependence on drugs – involves hour-by-hour use? Most other drugs stick around in the body long enough to require refills only every few hours (the single notable exception being crack cocaine, which is used as often as possible until the supply is gone).

Of course, addiction isn't the only reason people continue to smoke, but it's generally the main one.

Smoking meets your emotional needs

Why do you smoke now? Probably for numerous reasons, the biggest of which is that you are addicted and can't stop (see preceding section). Here are some other possible reasons:

- ✔ You use nicotine as a remedy for anxiety.

- ✔ To you, smoking is an escape from this world and a window into another world; smoking shuts down your mind, if only for a moment.

- ✔ A cigarette gives you confidence.

Stressful situations may encourage you to reach for a cigarette. Find other ways to deal with stress.

Smoking, like any addiction, is not only about putting off thoughts about the risks of cigarettes. Like all addictions, it is about the murder of *now*. When you think about it, though, the act of smoking is a statement about the intolerability of the moment and about your (lack of) commitment to life.

You use smoking to control your weight

Yes, tobacco takes the edge off your appetite for food. Yes, millions of smokers use cigarettes and other tobacco products to replace food. Nicotine even gives you an edge, a feeling of being wired, that you don't get from food. For these reasons, many smokers lean on the excuse that they need to keep smoking to control their weight.

If weight gain is a concern for you, we're happy to tell you that most people who quit smoking don't gain more than 5 kilograms. The rest is up to you, meaning that you need to think of weight gain – if you experience it at all – as strictly temporary and as something that you can remedy. It's a matter of priorities.

Gaining several kilograms for a relatively short period won't kill you. Continuing to smoke might.

Good nutrition is important in losing or maintaining your weight. You can help yourself feel more fit, trim, and healthy. Your physical engine runs much more smoothly and efficiently on a mix of protein and fruit and vegetable carbohydrates than it does on fat-loaded fast foods. Eating a healthy, nutritious diet gives you more energy, which is something you may have relied on cigarettes for. If you're overweight, you can find excellent resources in books and on the Internet. Highly trained professionals, such as nutritionists, dieticians, and personal trainers, can review your food intake and exercise schedule and help you devise an optimal plan. For more information on good eating, check out *Nutrition For Dummies*, by Nigel Denby, Sue Baic, and Carol Ann Rinzler (Wiley).

Plenty of liquids are highly recommended when you stop smoking. Some people feel that the more (healthy) liquids you drink during your initial days of stopping, the better. Water, fruit juice, and herbal teas are fine.

Some newbie quitters find that it helps to carry around a bag of celery or carrot sticks to munch on throughout the day. Gum chewing (sugarless, unless you're looking to give your dentist more business) is an old standby as an over-the-counter replacement for smokers.

You use smoking to control stress

For many people, smoking is a remedy for anxiety and stress. Although nicotine in low doses is a stimulant that temporarily boosts your alertness and ability to concentrate, higher doses act as a sedative, relaxing you and dumbing down your neuromuscular system. Smoking does relieve stress, but it *adds* to stress in many ways.

What's the point of reducing stress with cigarettes when each cigarette heightens your risk for disease, makes you feel guilty, and causes you aesthetic and financial discomfort? Aesthetic discomfort? You may call this sensation guilt. Whatever you call the feeling of having succumbed to the craving for a smoke, the feeling is usually unpleasant.

Quitting is the time to exercise, take walks, play sports, take up a new hobby, and spend time with other people. If certain activities are particularly relaxing or rewarding for you, by all means pursue them. On the other hand, if certain activities are particularly stressful and usually make you reach for a cigarette, avoid them as much as possible, especially during your first week of stopping.

The amount and degree of stress in your life is also a factor in determining how much of an addictive personality you have. Fortunately, your stress level is somewhat under your control. You can work towards changing your internal and external environments if they are significant sources of stress for you.

Teenagers: Smoking to Be Cool

Teenagers often begin smoking because their parents and friends, and the film and TV stars they idolise, smoke. You can have a positive impact on young people's developing selves by pointing out examples of extremely successful, cool people who make a point of taking great care of their health, and by setting a good example yourself.

Presenting kids with mixed messages is a universal problem. Parents and other adults who smoke and then ask their children not to are asking younger people to conform to a standard that they themselves can't achieve. Not fair! One of the great (and very serious) aspects of being young is that you expect people to play by the rules.

Kids expect their parents by and large to live by their parents' own stated rules. If you don't want your child to smoke, don't let them know that it's really okay by smoking yourself!

Another common reason that teenagers smoke is peer pressure. Adolescence is a time in life when the pressure to conform, to fit in, is unbelievably intense. For many kids, smoking is a passive form of compliance with the group. Teenage smokers are likely to have friends who also smoke.

Stopping smoking may need to involve quitting a particular social circle as well. Sometimes it isn't enough for a teenager to say no. Teenagers whose friends are notorious smokers, drinkers, and party-goers may need to choose new friends. It can be done!

Teenagers are always trying to establish and declare their identities. Often, this effort involves attempts to define themselves as distinct from their parents and their parents' generation. In more extreme cases, kids become rebellious and defiant. For some teens, speaking out and being different is more important than being healthy or making realistic plans for the future, which can lead them to try things like smoking.

Understanding the Effects of Nicotine on Your Brain

Part of understanding why you smoke is understanding the brain circuitry involved. When you understand how the brain works in normal health, without any drugs or smoke, you're in a better position to recognise the effects that tampering with the system (that is, by adding tobacco) has on the brain.

The complexity of the adult human brain is staggering: It's so finely tuned that its workings and architecture are almost beyond description. Nonetheless, decades of research have succeeded in identifying some of the major information pipelines in the brain. The adult brain weighs only 1.3–1.4 kilograms but, oh, what a kilo or so it is!

Your brain contains 2–3 billion *neurons,* or nerve cells, each of which is connected to one or more other neurons, making for billions upon billions of *synapses* (connections) in the organ. The possibilities of information flow are nearly endless.

Neurons communicate with each other electrically and chemically. Once an *action potential* (a wave of electricity) sweeps down the trunk of a nerve cell, it depolarises the cell membrane, causing a flow of ions such as potassium and sodium through special channels in the cell membrane. Next, chemical packets of neurotransmitters are released from the nerve terminal across the *synaptic space* (the gap between nerve cells), where they trigger receptors on the surface of the next neuron in the sequence. You can think of the arrangement as an elaborate, effective bucket brigade on a microscopic scale. See Figure 2-1 for an illustration of the arrangement.

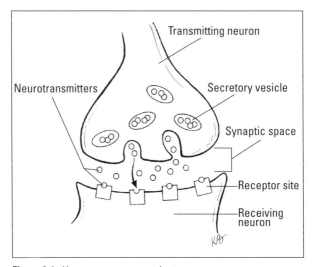

Figure 2-1: How neurons communicate.

A great deal has been said, and will continue to be said, about these neurotransmitters. The main neurotransmitters – acetylcholine, serotonin, norepinephrine, and dopamine – work alongside a number of other chemical transmitters that have additional functions and may work to antagonise or boost the effects of the better-known ones.

The brain is like a symphony. To sound right, all the different instruments must play together.

Nicotine hits neuroreceptors. It is known to have major effects on acetylcholine (nicotinic) receptors, and there is strong evidence that nicotine affects dopamine receptors as well. Dopamine receptors, in turn, may be involved in the brain's feel-good system. Nicotine and other addictive substances may be so habit-forming, at least in part, because they trigger the brain's own reward system, and when the brain feels good, it wants to keep on feeling good.

There's more to smoke than just nicotine. Tobacco smoke contains hundreds of chemicals in addition to nicotine.

Recent research using brain imaging suggests that tobacco smoke may contain psychoactive chemicals in addition to nicotine. Research has also shown that some of these 'fellow traveller' chemicals can affect the way you feel and behave. A number of the other chemicals that go along for the ride in cigarette smoke have potent effects on the brain and behaviour.

Drugs like nicotine that are highly rewarding to the brain because of their relaxing, distracting, energising, and appetite-suppressing properties actually condition users to want more.

Chapter 3

Evaluating the Health Risks of Smoking

. . . .

In This Chapter

▶ Blocking the pathway to breathing

▶ Looking at risk, organ by organ

▶ Reversing the damage

. . . .

*E*very breath of clean air you take is filled with healthy, life-giving oxygen, nitrogen, and other gases. Every puff of tobacco you take is packed with poisonous chemicals and gases, including tars, carbon monoxide, and carcinogenic hydrocarbons.

You probably already know that smoking is bad for you – that fact is hard to avoid. But if you still smoke, even though you know it's harmful, understanding the damage that smoking does to your body may help you. Knowing the specifics just may be what it takes to get you to decide to stop *now*.

Damaging the Respiratory System

The respiratory system is the area where smoking does the majority of damage. For example, smokers are at much higher risk than non-smokers of developing cancer and other diseases of the head and neck. Conditions that smokers often suffer from include:

✔ **Lung cancer:** Millions of people die from lung cancer. This is the most common form of cancer in the world, with approximately 34,000 people dying of the disease each year in the UK. Worryingly, 90 per cent of lung cancers are due to the effects of smoking.

A persistent cough, coughing up blood-stained phlegm, or a chest infection that does not get better are some of the symptoms of lung cancer and should be checked by your GP.

✔ **Gingivitis:** *Gingivitis,* an inflammation of the gums that causes pain and bleeding, is fairly common among smokers. It is due, as are most of the respiratory ailments that smokers fall victim to, to constant irritation from tar and other toxins in tobacco smoke.

✔ **Laryngeal cancer:** Chances are that the person you noticed with a mechanical voice-box (an artificial larynx) had his or her larynx removed due to cancer.

Some symptoms of laryngeal cancer include a persistent cough, hoarseness or voice changes, a lump in the neck, and breathing problems.

✔ **Chronic obstructive pulmonary disease (COPD):**
COPD is very difficult to treat and is irreversible.
The most effective way to halt the progression of
COPD is to quit smoking. COPD is also known as
chronic bronchitis and emphysema:

- *Bronchitis* is an inflammation of the delicate
  mucous membrane lining the *bronchi* – a pair
  of large tubes branching off from the trachea
  (windpipe) – resulting in irritation, pain,
  coughing, and excess mucus.

- *Emphysema* is another heartbreaker, involving
  the progressive loss of elasticity of lung tissue.
  A person with emphysema can inhale but has
  greater and greater trouble exhaling. As a
  result, the *alveoli* (tiny air sacs in the lungs)
  and lung tissue essentially expand, blow up,
  and blow out, creating larger and ever less
  functional ventilation space. People with
  emphysema literally struggle to breathe.

✔ **Asthma:** *Asthma* is a condition that often arises in
childhood and involves the constriction, or tighten-
ing, of the bronchi and bronchioles, effectively
reducing the amount of air that can be taken in.
Smoking aggravates underlying asthma and can provoke episodes of asthmatic breathing in those who
have the illness. Asthma can be life-threatening.
Fortunately, medical care is usually effective and
provides fast relief.

✔ **Carbon monoxide poisoning:** Carbon monoxide is a
colourless, odourless gas that's found in car exhaust
fumes and cigarette smoke, among other things. You
don't want to breathe in carbon monoxide, because
it competes with oxygen. The amazing molecule

haemoglobin is the oxygen carrier in red blood cells, moving oxygen from your lungs to the rest of your body. When you smoke or you are exposed to carbon monoxide in some other way, such as in an unventilated car, the carbon monoxide binds much more readily to the haemoglobin molecules, and the level of oxygen in your blood can drop dramatically.

If you've ever smoked too many cigarettes in too short a time, you may have experienced acute oxygen deprivation as a result of carbon monoxide overload. Carbon monoxide poisoning can be fatal. The symptoms of carbon monoxide overload can include hyperventilation, a fast irregular heart rate, confusion, drowsiness, and difficulty breathing.

Smoking Out the Health Risks of Tobacco

You've surely got the idea that tobacco in any form is bad for your health, as well as for your wallet. Not a single organ or organ system in your body is unaffected by exposure to smoke, particularly chronic exposure, but many people are unaware of the far-reaching effects that tobacco products have on the rest of the body. The following sections describe some of those effects.

Smoke gets in your eyes (and mouth and heart and lungs)

The physical and medical consequences of smoking are numerous, and the extent and seriousness of smoking-related illness is shocking. Cigarette smoking is the single

Adding up the damage

Damage to the lungs and bronchi caused by smoking accumulates over time. If you get sick from smoking, the illness results from longstanding and repeated injury to the delicate respiratory tract lining. The good news is that once you stop smoking, your lungs and bronchi instantly go to work to heal themselves.

biggest cause of cancer in the world. One in four deaths in the UK is from smoking-related cancer. Approximately another 11,000 more people die as a result of exposure to smoke in the environment (known as second-hand smoke).

Smokers die at younger ages than non-smokers, too. According to the World Health Organization, half of regular smokers who began smoking during adolescence die as a result of their tobacco use.

Cancer is one of the worst effects that smoking has on the body. Organs that have direct contact with tobacco smoke – the throat, lungs, and oesophagus – are the most likely to develop cancer. Here are some of the other effects you are likely to experience if you continue your habit (if you aren't experiencing them already):

✔ Your fingers and fingernails become discoloured with tarry, mustard-hued stains that can't be scrubbed off.

✔ Your breath smells like the cigarette or cigar you're smoking, or old, lingering tobacco.

- ✔ Over time, your skin takes on the appearance of advanced age, with exaggerated wrinkles, crevices, and worry lines.

- ✔ Your gums and teeth suffer, with periodontal disease, including gingivitis. Teeth become stained in unwelcome shades ranging from mustard yellow to dark brown.

- ✔ Cigarettes are implicated in the development of *osteoporosis,* a thinning or weakening of the bones.

- ✔ Female smokers over the age of 35 who take oral contraceptives (the pill) are at greater risk of heart attack, stroke, and blood clots.

- ✔ Smoking aggravates conditions such as obesity, high blood pressure, and diabetes, which can lead to more severe symptoms and/or greater need for treatment.

- ✔ At least one in eight cases of high blood pressure is due to smoking.

- ✔ Babies of mothers who smoke are at greater risk of sudden infant death syndrome (SIDS).

- ✔ Children of mothers who smoke during pregnancy stand a greater chance of having asthma, ear infections, and upper respiratory tract infections.

Smoking is also one of the major risk factors for developing cardiovascular disease, including heart disease, stroke, abdominal aortic aneurysm, and impaired circulation to the extremities. Cardiovascular disease is the number-one cause of death in the Western world. The more you smoke, the greater your risk of getting some form of this disease.

Smokers are almost twice as likely as non-smokers to have a heart attack.

Cigarettes and cancer: A match made in heaven

Cigarette smoke contains dozens of *carcinogens* (cancer-causing chemical compounds), such as nitrosamines, aldehydes, and aromatic hydrocarbons. Despite the cigarette companies' decades-long advertising crusade, there's no doubt that smoking causes lung cancer, which is the number-one cause of cancer mortality. Experts note that 90 per cent of lung cancer is related to smoking.

A smoker's odds of developing lung cancer are 12–22 times higher than a non-smoker's. The more you smoke (including the number of cigarettes, the depth of the inhale, and the number of years of smoking), the greater your chance of developing lung cancer.

Lung cancer isn't the only cancer caused by smoking. Cancer of the larynx is usually caused by smoking, as is oral (mouth) cancer, oesophageal cancer (four out of five cases are caused by smoking), kidney cancer, and bladder cancer. Up to a third of pancreatic cancer deaths are caused by cigarette smoking, and smokers have a significantly increased chance of developing stomach cancer, cancer of the cervix (in women), and leukaemia.

The good news is that you can translate your new-found awareness into immediate action. The moment you stop smoking, your body begins to clean and repair itself.

Nicotine puts your body on high alert

Within seconds of the first puff of tobacco, your heart rate, blood pressure, and breathing rate increase. Your body is immediately stimulated, releasing adrenaline, which puts it in a state of readiness for fight or flight. All body systems are put on high alert; you remain in physiological high gear, with increased heart rate and blood pressure, whenever you are smoking – and for some hours after – until the nicotine leaves your system. As you can imagine, a continued stress response is harmful to the body.

Nicotine has other immediate effects. You probably remember the very first time or two you tried to smoke, because you probably coughed, retched, or became quite nauseated. Nausea is a direct effect of nicotine.

One to 12 hours after the last cigarette, confirmed smokers begin to experience nicotine withdrawal symptoms. These symptoms include:

- ✔ Irritability
- ✔ Fatigue
- ✔ Mood swings
- ✔ Insomnia or hypersomnia (too much sleep)
- ✔ Trouble concentrating
- ✔ Headache
- ✔ Increased appetite
- ✔ Anxiety
- ✔ Depression
- ✔ Shifting energy levels

Interestingly, many of these symptoms are similar to symptoms that arise with depression and other types of mood disorders, which may help explain why Zyban, an antidepressant drug available only on prescription, helps some newly abstinent smokers through the process of stopping. See Chapter 5 for more on Zyban and other therapies that lessen nicotine withdrawal symptoms.

The cardiovascular system

Repeated doses of nicotine cause a general overload of the nervous and cardiovascular systems. Blood vessels, particularly arteries and smaller arteries called *arterioles,* clamp down in response to this repeated chemical assault. Narrower, constricted blood vessels lead to elevated blood pressure and a greater likelihood of obstructions to circulation, eventually leading to permanent obstruction. (See Chapter 2 for a detailed discussion of nicotine's effects on the brain.)

Long-term constriction of blood vessels and increased blood pressure lead to fatty deposits that form right beneath the delicate inner lining of blood vessels. These *atheromas* clog the pipes and may end up as a life-threatening blockage in an artery of the heart or brain.

Just 24 hours after stopping smoking, carbon dioxide is eliminated from your system, and tar starts to clear from your lungs. One year after stopping smoking, your risk of a heart attack is halved.

The immune system

Your body performs remarkable waste management services 24/7. Defender white blood cells *(macrophages)* continually engulf and gobble up foreign matter, such as dust, soot, and noxious fumes, keeping these toxic particles from further contact with the tissues. At the same time, white blood cells called *lymphocytes* recognise foreign matter and fight it with antibodies or other molecules. These antibodies tag invaders – such as viruses – as 'foreign', and lead to their later ingestion by the white blood cells.

Smokers often suffer from frequent or persistent infections, such as upper respiratory tract infections and colds, because their immune systems are overwhelmed by constant toxins and chemicals from nicotine.

Some people are allergic to components of tobacco and tobacco smoke. The allergic response takes many forms, from a few sneezes to an all-out and potentially life-threatening rash, difficulty breathing, and even systemic shock.

The gastrointestinal and genitourinary systems

When you use tobacco, you end up swallowing the smoke, tobacco, and associated particulate matter. As a consequence, your stomach lining is repeatedly exposed to the harmful ingredients of tobacco. The gastric lining *(mucosa)* of your stomach can react to repeated contact with tobacco carcinogens such as nitrosamines and free radicals by forming mutated (cancerous) cells. In addition, the adrenaline boost that comes with each puff can eventually lead to the breakdown of the gastric lining and to peptic ulcer disease.

The constituents of tobacco smoke that make it from your lungs into your bloodstream pass through your kidneys, which filter the blood and excrete these toxins into the urine. Urine that contains carcinogens sits in the bladder for hours at a time – a setup for bladder cancer.

Had enough? There's more. Your liver, which is the recycling plant of your body, ordinarily breaks down *(metabolises)* the thousands of chemical compounds, including tobacco compounds, that pass through your gut and bloodstream every day. Complex chemical compounds found in cigarettes activate enzymatic rubbish-removal systems in the liver, making the liver more effective as a waste recycler. It's not a good thing, however, as it results in an increased ability to break down other chemical compounds, such as prescribed medication, too quickly.

Smokers often need higher doses of medication than non-smokers because their livers break down medications more rapidly.

Your skin

Just one puff of smoke encourages the release of millions and millions of free radicals that circulate throughout your body creating carnage. These free radicals, along with the 4,000 toxins from cigarette smoke, cause your skin to age prematurely by reducing the collagen in your skin. The effects of smoking literally cause your skin to suffocate by restricting and reducing the oxygen levels in the blood, producing a grey, ashen complexion.

No amount of anti-ageing cream will help prevent the wrinkles around the mouth and eyes, so common on a smoker's face.

Mental effects

Curiously, the mental effects of tobacco, at least in lower doses, are stimulating. Tobacco's stimulating effect explains why many smokers practice *titration,* or blending of sedatives like alcohol with nicotine. They take themselves up with cigarettes and lower themselves back down with drinks.

At higher doses, nicotine acts as a sedative on the central nervous system by occupying and triggering brain receptors, resulting in nicotine poisoning, which can lead to nausea, vomiting, convulsions, and even death.

Smoker's cough

If you notice one thing about a smoker it's the cough. It's full of phlegm. Due to the death of the mucus-moving ciliated cells and the goblet cells that protect the delicate airway walls, the mucus irritates the cough receptors, and the trapped smoke irritates the airways, causing cells to change shape. One in five smokers suffers with a persistent cough, but at least 75 per cent of those with a persistent cough don't realise that they could have a fatal lung disease, COPD.

COPD kills 30,000 people in the UK every year. The choking fits, the coughing, the harshness of the taste, the exposure of the delicate mucus membranes in your mouth, throat, and lungs to toxins – what's the point? Just hope that you don't get to the point where smoking is grossly damaging your health.

If you're concerned about a cough, pain, or any other aspect of breathing, consult a doctor.

If you have any medical problems now, such as hypertension, obesity, asthma, diabetes, or a peptic ulcer, smoking is likely to aggravate these problems.

Quitting While You're Ahead

Evidence suggests that your lungs' ability to expand and inhale and exhale properly returns over time when you stop smoking. All your body systems, including the circulatory system, the immune system (white blood cells), and the lymphatic system (part of your body's defence network), go into mop-up mode and remove or cordon off as many of the tobacco toxins and damaged cells as possible.

In fact, within 20 minutes of stopping smoking, there are positive health changes and, after 2 days of stopping smoking, your lungs start to clear, and your sense of taste and smell starts to return.

According to statistics, if you're 65 and female, quitting smoking now will add about four years to your life. Those who quit by the age of 35 live an average of 7–8½ years longer than those who keep on smoking. Women who quit before pregnancy or within the first three months of pregnancy, lower their risk of miscarriage and of having a low-birth-weight baby to the risk levels of non-smoking women.

Second chance

What happens when you stop smoking?

After 20 minutes, your blood pressure and pulse rate return to normal.

After 24 hours, the carbon monoxide is removed from your body.

After 48 hours, the nicotine is expelled from your body.

Between 2 and 21 weeks, your circulation improves.

After one year, your risk of a heart attack falls to half that of a non-smoker.

After ten years, your risk of lung cancer falls.

Part II
Packing It In

'So, you wish to stop smoking
— come in and sit down.'

In this part . . .

This part enables you to have a really good look at the ways to stop smoking. Stopping smoking is not just about saying no, and it doesn't have to be a matter of grim determination and white knuckles. It involves the informed, active, and ongoing use of quitting tools. We talk about those tools here.

The part also encourages you to have a good long think about how you might go about changing your mind about smoking and remaining smoke free. This part gives you an in-depth look at the ammunition currently available in the war to reclaim your body and your health.

Chapter 4

Just Stopping

In This Chapter

▶ Breaking your bond with tobacco

▶ Going cold turkey

▶ Letting go of a bad habit

▶ Finding something better

▶ Learning from your mistakes

*T*raditional methods of stopping smoking include going cold turkey or gradually reducing the amount you smoke. Fortunately, there are many ways that you can choose to quit smoking. The most important thing is to stop smoking and soon. Planning is important, but so is action. The way that you choose to stop doesn't matter; stopping does.

Planning a Date

The consensus is that your plan to stop should be made as carefully and in as much detail as possible. You want to avoid an impulsive attempt to stop, because you don't want to give in to impulses – you don't want a quitting impulse to be followed by a smoking impulse.

Mark your calendar. The day you choose to stop is a special day. On that day, you take back control of your life and begin to breathe freely. Your body and cells begin to rid themselves of the accumulated toxins of tobacco and renew themselves with vitality, energy, and oxygen.

The day that you pick to stop smoking is a great day, so mark the occasion. Some people find that choosing a symbolic day, such as New Year's Day, helps, but no matter what day you choose, it will be special to you. Remember to let your family and friends know about this date too, so that they can help support you.

Go beyond picking your stopping day. Work out the specifics of how you will spend that day. Will it be a work day? With whom will you spend the day? Having a plan, and knowing what to expect, makes dealing with this often difficult (but great!) day much easier.

When temptation gets in the way, as no doubt it will, make sure you have some strategies ready and waiting. A strategy may be something simple like getting up and changing your surroundings, or it may be doing some exercise or having a piece of chewing gum or fruit. Stuck for ideas? Chapter 11 offers some substitution suggestions.

Quitting smoking is an excellent thing to do. It's one of the greatest gifts you can give yourself.

Letting Go

Letting go of smoking can be one of the biggest and scariest steps you take in your life. You become accustomed to doing things in a certain way. You become accustomed to smoking a certain number of cigarettes at particular times of day. You quickly get used to the taste, rhythm, and feel of lighting up. The act of striking a match and lighting up a cigarette becomes a kind of ritual – a regular part of your life. When you think of going about your life from morning until night, you think of having a smoke. Cigarettes are the constant accompaniment to both work and time at home.

Letting cigarettes go is difficult. Change is hard. Scientists who study change have noted that even a positive change, such as getting a promotion, moving to a nicer place, or getting married, can be stressful. There's something reassuring about a habit, no matter how destructive it can be in the long run. But that's what cigarettes are – destructive and habit-forming.

Dropping a bad habit is more important than understanding why you do it!

When you stop smoking, you're letting go of a dependency and a habit. You're letting go of an old and familiar way of doing and handling things. Instead of running away in your mind, feeling overwhelmed, or coming to the conclusion that you can't and won't cope with stopping, look at the individual components of your attachment – the physical, emotional, and mental.

> ✔ **Physical:** The physical component is the least of your concerns, because you can temporarily replace the nicotine in tobacco with a nicotine replacement therapy that minimises any withdrawal symptoms you may have. (See Chapter 5 for more on replacement therapies such as the nicotine patch and nicotine gum.)
>
> ✔ **Emotional:** Often described as a psychological craving, you may find that feelings of loss, deprivation, and nostalgia (among others) come up when you stop smoking. These feelings of bereavement are to

be expected. For many people, smoking is a constant companion, a 'friend' who is always available, who can always be relied on to make them feel a certain way. Who wouldn't feel saddened by the loss of this friend?

✔ **Mental:** The mental component is more complex. You're attached to the idea that you need and want a cigarette, particularly at certain times. This is called desire. The wish for a smoke is at the extreme end of the spectrum of desire, especially if you haven't had a smoke in a while. You get to the point where it's hard not to think about smoking. The urge presses you, prods you, until you finally give in. Or maybe you don't give in.

The first step to stopping smoking is not to give in to the desire for a smoke. See how great it feels to overcome what feels like an instinct, a reflex.

Don't be a slave to nicotine. Do something because you've made a decision to do it.

Stopping smoking is a serious pursuit. It's every bit as challenging and important to your survival as giving up any other unhealthy attachment.

Doing Without: The Cold-Turkey Method

When you think about the phrase *cold turkey,* you may envision some poor addicts, huddled and shivering in a corner of a miserable room, their eyes bulging as they pray for a grain of their drug. You've probably seen pictures, films, or TV programmes about the unfortunate souls – addicts, 'junkies' – who live through the gut-wrenching deprivation of their substance of dependence. Usually, these extreme scenarios are related to heroin or other opiate-based drugs, but withdrawal rears its ugly head with tobacco as well.

Stopping your use of tobacco won't kill you. Stopping will save your life. But, for a while, it may feel like it's going to kill you. Don't worry, it won't! You can stop. Millions of people already have and millions more will do so in the future.

To lessen the discomfort caused by withdrawal symptoms, try the following techniques:

- Take exercise.

- Find help from support groups, family, and friends.

- Use a nicotine replacement therapy (see Chapter 5).

Is cold turkey – stopping smoking suddenly and completely – the right approach for you? Most approaches endorse total cessation. If you take a more gradual approach, such as having the first cigarette of the day a little bit later each day, you run the risk of relapsing into old, familiar habits. The best, and perhaps only, way to find out whether cold turkey will work for you is to give it a try. If you find that you just can't say no, that's okay, too. There are many quitting tools and resources available to you now. There's no harm in trying – but don't give up! If the cold turkey method doesn't work for you, one of the many others will.

Helping your teenager say no to cigarettes

In a world where crack cocaine and other hard drugs seem almost common, it's easy to think that cigarettes are pretty harmless by comparison. Teenagers especially may come to this conclusion. But they need to understand that nicotine is a drug that can do serious damage. It acts directly on the nervous system, causing stimulation, sedation, excitability, and agitation. As Chapter 3 explains in detail, tobacco products can have devastating physical effects. For example, teenage girls who smoke increase their risk of developing breast cancer before they reach menopause. Smoking may also increase a person's chances of developing anxiety or depression. The best way to avoid breast cancer, lung disease, and other smoking-related illnesses is *prevention.* Don't smoke!

If teenagers needs further proof that nicotine is a powerful drug, get them to think and talk about what millions of people go through when they try to stop. Any drug that can cause such uncomfortable withdrawal symptoms must be powerful. It's far better not to smoke at all.

Resisting peer pressure is difficult for any teenager. The best way is for teenagers to be prepared with answers before the question is asked, so that when the time comes to say no, the right answer comes naturally. Teenagers can consider the following ways to say no:

- Thanks, but I'd rather live a full life.
- Thanks, but I'm allergic.
- I tried before and I didn't like it.
- Ever seen the inside of a smoker's lung?
- No, thanks.
- My cousin died of lung cancer.
- My grandfather has to suck on an oxygen tank because of smoking.
- I'm in training. Count me out.

Several thousand young people start smoking each day. Over time, millions of cases of tragic, unnecessary illness and death will result.

Cutting Back Gradually

Many people quit smoking by using the gradual method, also known as the *taper method*. No magic formula can determine the best amount by which you should reduce your daily tobacco intake (although many experts argue that stopping altogether is the best approach). Cutting down a bit at a time is sensible. If you smoke a pack a day, try smoking 18 cigarettes a day for the next week, then 16 a day for the next week, and so on.

You have set yourself a short-term goal that is attainable and, therefore, positive. Goals you reach aid your motivation. As for withdrawal symptoms, those who choose to cut back gradually often feel they suffer less from them or find they manage them better.

This downward progression may be too slow for you. The 'feeling' part of your brain will tell you 'Smoke more! Smoke more!'. But the *cognitive,* or rational, side of your brain can, and should, win out. Hang in there. Stick with it and you'll add years to your life.

How you quit doesn't really matter. When it comes to stopping smoking, the end justifies the means.

Giving It Up and Getting Rewards?

Something you hear quite often in the addiction treatment and recovery world – because it's true! – is that in order to give up a dependence, you need to take on a substitute. You (and everyone else) need something to replace whatever significant things you surrender in life.

So work out two or three specific substitutes or treats
that can immediately take the place of tobacco. For example, you may decide that for every day you don't smoke,
you will save £5 to buy new clothes or a personal training
session at the health club. Or you may save up for that
holiday of a lifetime. You may be surprised at how little
time it takes to save the money and just how much you
threw away on cigarettes.

There are thousands of substitute gratifications for
tobacco. See Chapter 11 if you'd like suggestions on
smoking substitutes.

Dealing with the Changes

As you move from what has been termed the *pre-
contemplator stage* to actually stopping, you go through
changes in a variety of areas: physical, emotional, financial, social, and spiritual. Some of the changes are painful
and involve struggle and a good deal of commitment on
your part; most of the changes are positive and excellent!
You have a lot to look forward to as you move from
planning to stopping. Here's what you can expect:

> ✔ The *physical* changes take place immediately and
> over the mid- and long-term as well. The acute or
> immediate changes following the cessation of
> tobacco use can include depression, anxiety, rest-
> lessness, jitteriness, increased appetite, and dimin-
> ished energy. Some people describe feeling wired or
> simultaneously wired and tired. These are the typi-
> cal withdrawal symptoms that many people who
> stop smoking experience.

✔ The e*motional* changes can include increased alertness (or increased tiredness), moodiness, irritability, and even depression and anxiety. One reason you smoke is to regulate your moods, to control how you feel. When you stop smoking, your brain's emotional circuits go on rebound activity, and you may feel the opposite of the way you feel when you light up. These emotional changes are mostly temporary. However, on a positive note, the feelings of guilt you might experience every time you light up disappear. All those guilt trips that took up so much of your time, energy, and emotion are wiped out the minute you stop. Within a matter of weeks, you will feel better, more alert, more vital, and better able to handle whatever stresses life may throw at you.

✔ The *financial* changes that accompany quitting smoking are all for the good. You'll save at least £4–5 a day if you smoked a pack a day. You'll have the satisfaction of having more money to spend and of knowing that your decision to stop smoking put that extra money in your pocket.

Evaluating What Went Wrong

This may be your first attempt to stop or it may be the 14th. Don't be discouraged; millions of people all over the world have succeeded at stopping smoking. Most of those who have quit had tried several times, before making it last.

Many people have succeeded at quitting on their first try – you can too!

Just because you tried to stop smoking in the past and failed doesn't mean that you can't succeed now. Most people who stop successfully try to quit up to a half a dozen times before succeeding. Use whatever resources are currently available to you to increase your chances of stopping.

The first thing you need to do is work out what made you relapse to smoking in the past. If you can recall the specific triggers that made you pick up smoking again, you can be extra wary of them and plan for them. In this way, you are able to deal with the triggers before they get to you.

Not sure what caused your relapse? Consider these common triggers:

- ✓ **Believing that you've got the habit licked.** You may have felt that you could have just one cigarette. Shortly after, you may have convinced yourself that having just one more would cause little harm. By the third cigarette, you were as addicted as before.

- ✓ **Catastrophising.** You slipped and had one or more cigarettes despite your best intentions. You felt so guilty, like you'd let yourself down so much, that you threw up your hands in despair and essentially gave up. 'I may as well enjoy myself' is the theme song that accompanies this self-pitying wail.

- ✓ **Stressing.** An event occurs in your world and you panic: 'I've got to have a cigarette.' Actually, you don't have to have a cigarette. Having a cigarette only amplifies your stress. (See Chapter 3 to find out how smoking revs up your body.) Not only do you still need to deal with whatever is taking place in your life, but you now have additional stressful stimuli such as a rapid heartbeat, coughing, and a bitter, smoky taste in your mouth, not to mention the supremely unpleasant feeling of self-betrayal.

Stopping smoking can't come even remotely close to killing you. Cigarette smoking can kill you, however.

✔ **Relaxing.** Being on holiday or kicking back on a weekend day is the perfect excuse to have a cool drink and light up. *Wrong.* Take a closer look at what relaxing is all about. Letting down your hair and unwinding has to do with smelling the roses, feeling the cool breeze, and every other form of slowing down and feeling good. Cigarettes are not about slowing down. Cigarettes are stimulants that kick up your pulse rate and blood pressure and rob you of your time that much more quickly.

✔ **Watching other people smoke.** You may think, 'If they can smoke without consequences, why can't I?' You feel sorry for yourself because you have to give up something you like. Giving up smoking is letting go of an oral fixation that you really don't need. The path towards health involves taking care of your whole body and your whole mind. You do so by attending carefully to yourself: You find a workout that makes you feel good; you find new ways to think, look at things, and behave, that are consistent with the person you want to be.

✔ **Accepting substandard health.** You may already have a cough or congestion in your lungs first thing in the morning. Following this line of logic, you may try to convince yourself that the damage is already done, so why not at least enjoy the cigarettes?

✔ **Being tired of feeling tired.** It's true that cigarettes give you a lift, but only temporarily. Like any drug, you need to increase the amount to obtain the same effect. However, stopping smoking will add enormously to your available energy after the first few weeks.

Zyban, the anti-craving medication, helps control the fatigue that can accompany nicotine withdrawal. (Hop over to Chapter 5 for more details on Zyban.) Exercise, good sleep habits, and a positive, enthusiastic outlook also contribute to a high-energy life.

✔ **Trying to control your weight.** Maybe smoking did stop you from putting something else in your mouth, but healthy eating habits combined with exercise will stop you from putting on weight. (See Chapter 8 for further details on healthy eating.) Look around you: Countless numbers of people who don't smoke manage to remain slim.

Think back to a time when quitting didn't work. Where were you? What were you doing at the time you broke down and smoked? Who were you with? People, places, activities, and time can be triggers, too. Plan ahead if you know you may encounter these again.

Evidence suggests that using nicotine replacement therapies increases your chances of quitting. See Chapter 5 for more information about nicotine replacement therapies.

The power of hypnosis and positive thinking

The power of the mind is no joke. Libraries are full of books about the power of positive thinking. Hypnotherapy is often successfully used as an aid to stop smoking, while neuro-linguistic programming can change the way you think and feel about smoking.

Hypnosis offers deep, trance-like relaxation, and the power of suggestion. When you delve into the history of hypnosis, it becomes less and less clear what hypnosis actually is. Don't worry: Sometimes you don't have to understand how or why something works in order for it to work!

Neuro-linguistic programming, on the other hand, uses modern psychotherapy to monitor and adapt your thinking so that you can change your negative thoughts and beliefs for positive ones.

Both techniques work on the theory that the power of your own mind is capable of changing your habits. (See Chapter 6 for further details.)

In fact, hypnotherapy is considered a powerful tool for smokers who want to quit, and some die-hard smokers have been know to need only one session of hypnotherapy to help them stop. One of the main advantages of using hypnotherapy to stop smoking is that there are no side-effects, no drugs to take, and in a return a huge boost of confidence and self-esteem, so it's worth thinking about.

If you want to learn more about hypnotherapy and positive thinking then *Hypnotherapy For Dummies,* by Mike Bryant and Peter Mabbutt (Wiley), and *Neuro-linguistic Programming For Dummies,* by Romilla Ready and Kate Burton (Wiley), may be useful to you.

Hypnotherapy isn't just about helping you to stop smoking – it's also about helping you to stay a non-smoker. Right now, you can surrender and cower in fear of your life without tobacco, or, through focusing your actions, educating yourself, and using hypnosis and/or harnessing the power of positive thinking, you can stop smoking for good.

Neuro-linguistic programming encourages you to change negative thoughts and self-doubts for positive affirmations, so that every action or behaviour you exhibit has positive intent. It's about making real-life changes to achieve the results you want. Okay, so you are not going to become a non-smoker overnight, and you may have to think about it and work at it, but that applies to anything you really want to achieve. You may give up overnight, but the desire for a cigarette is another issue completely, and to win that war you may have to learn to think differently about smoking. Neuro-linguistic programming helps you take charge of your life and the decisions you make.

Chapter 5

Using Nicotine Replacement Therapies

In This Chapter

▶ Replacing tobacco with safer nicotine

▶ Patching up your health with over-the-counter quitting aids

▶ Making use of nicotine inhalers, aerosols, and lozenges

▶ Exploring prescription-only NRT options

▶ Conquering cravings with Zyban

▶ Combining NRTs and Zyban

*T*his chapter discusses over-the-counter and prescription medications, powerful tools that help smokers quit. Although these nicotine replacement therapies, or NRTs, contain nicotine, they are far safer than tobacco, as the nicotine in them is released in a slow and controlled manner. Effective stop-smoking programmes usually involve a variety of supports and tools, including NRTs, anti-craving medications such as Zyban, and group support.

If you decide to use an NRT, especially an over-the-counter one, make sure to read the package inserts and instructions very carefully. If used incorrectly, these products can have serious side effects.

Exploring Nicotine Replacement Therapies

A *nicotine replacement therapy* (NRT) is just what it sounds like: a therapy that does its job by replacing the nicotine you'd normally get by smoking. When you use nicotine replacement therapy, you are preventing and treating nicotine withdrawal symptoms, but you aren't smoking. The NRT delivers a measured amount of nicotine to your body at regular intervals. This is one of the great benefits of nicotine replacement therapy: You minimise the discomforts of withdrawal without having to smoke.

Symptoms of nicotine withdrawal include:

- ✔ Fatigue
- ✔ Hyperactivity
- ✔ Anxiety
- ✔ Restlessness
- ✔ Difficulty concentrating
- ✔ Depression
- ✔ Irritability
- ✔ Preoccupation with smoking
- ✔ Excessive eating

If you are physically addicted to nicotine, using NRT has been shown to almost double your chances of successfully quitting smoking.

Nicotine replacement therapies are healthier than tobacco, because you eliminate the hundreds of toxic ingredients of smoke (except nicotine). Nicotine replacement therapies also contain far less of the by-products of the combustion of tobacco such as the particularly toxic free radicals and aerosolised polyaromatic hydrocarbons that can wreak havoc on cell growth and cause cancer. Plus, the NRT delivers a measured amount of nicotine to your body at regular intervals. Knowing how much nicotine you're taking in enables you to *titrate,* or carefully monitor and eventually decrease, the amount of nicotine you're getting.

Currently, researchers don't know whether one NRT is more effective than another. Likewise, they have not yet discovered whether one NRT has more or fewer side effects than another. What is certain is that there is no black-and-white formula that works for everybody.

There is no magic bullet for stopping smoking, but NRTs, as well as the non-NRT drugs Zyban and Champix, increase your chances of successfully stopping smoking fourfold.

Using NRTs Safely

Because nicotine replacement therapy – whatever form it takes – utilises actual nicotine, you need to take certain precautions:

✔ If you have a history of heart disease, vascular (circulation) problems, chest pain, hypertension, thyroid problems, or diabetes, discuss your quitting strategy with your doctor.

✔ NRTs are not suitable for anyone under the age of 18, unless prescribed by a doctor.

✔ If you are pregnant, check with your midwife before starting any kind of nicotine replacement therapy.

✔ Don't use nicotine replacement therapy if you know that you aren't ready to stop smoking.

Remember that nicotine is a powerful drug that acts on the brain. If you take in too much nicotine, regardless of the source, you experience a nicotine overdose.

Nicotine overdose can trigger the following symptoms:

✔ Dizziness

✔ Nausea

✔ Light-headedness

✔ Irregular or pounding heartbeat

✔ Acute anxiety

Using a nicotine replacement therapy such as the nicotine patch or gum and smoking at the same time is a perfect example of a way to overload on nicotine.

Trying Over-the-Counter NRTs

There are a variety of nicotine replacement therapies to choose from – patches, lozenges, inhalers, nasal sprays, microtabs, and nicotine gum. How you decide on the therapy best suited to you depends upon the type of smoker you are. Discuss the options with your GP or a smoking cessation counsellor. The NHS provides individual or group support by phone, text message, post or in person at a Stop Smoking Service. Your GP will be able to advise you.

Using the nicotine patch

The patch is known as a *transdermal* nicotine delivery system because the nicotine on its surface is slowly absorbed through your skin and into your bloodstream. (Cigarettes are the fastest nicotine delivery system. When you inhale, within seconds the nicotine in the cigarette smoke hits your bloodstream and then reaches your brain. With the patch, it takes a little longer.)

A constant, albeit low, amount of nicotine is delivered to your body throughout the day.

When you smoke, the level of nicotine in your body fluctuates a great deal, shooting up when you are smoking and decreasing between cigarettes. Falling nicotine levels cause withdrawal symptoms. The patch prevents these withdrawal symptoms from developing by providing a steady supply of nicotine while you wear it.

The patch needs to be placed on dry, non-hairy skin; the upper arm, for example, is a popular choice.

The patch supplies nicotine over a 16-hour or 24-hour period and comes in three different strengths. You are recommended to use these patches for up to three months, depending on the brand you choose. Generally speaking, you start with the patch that's right for you and wear it daily for six weeks. Then you drop to the next-lowest strength for the following two weeks, and then to the lowest strength for the final two weeks. Read the manufacturer's instructions for the product that you choose to make sure that you use the product correctly and safely.

Be sure to consult with your doctor before using the patch if you have any of the following conditions:

- High blood pressure not controlled with medication
- Depression
- Asthma
- Heart disease
- Heart palpitations (or some other form of irregular heartbeat)
- A previous heart attack
- Pregnancy

Do not smoke or use any other tobacco product while using the patch. The nicotine from cigarettes or other tobacco products together with the nicotine from the patch results in dangerously high levels of nicotine in the blood. The main side effects to watch out for with the patch are dizziness, rapid heartbeat or palpitations, insomnia, nausea, vomiting, headaches, and skin irritation. If you develop any of these symptoms, contact your doctor right away.

Some people find that skin irritation and itching diminish if they switch to a different brand of patch. Sleep disruption can be treated by switching from the 24-hour patch to the 16-hour patch.

The patch is a just a tool. You still have to practise right thinking and use every lifestyle strategy available to you to beat smoking.

Keep these points in mind when using the patch:

- ✔ You can bathe or swim while wearing the patch.

- ✔ Never use more than one patch simultaneously.

- ✔ Don't let children or animals touch or lick the patch.

- ✔ If the patch you're wearing falls off, put on a new one.

- ✔ Try to put on the day's patch at the same time each day in order to regularise your nicotine replacement therapy.

- ✔ Do not smoke while using the patch.

Chewing cravings away with nicotine gum

Nicotine gum (nicotine polacrilex) is a popular nicotine replacement therapy. Available over the counter, gum is easy to use and provides regular measured amounts of nicotine to the bloodstream. The gum is loaded with nicotine that's released slowly yet absorbed rapidly by the blood-rich mucous membranes of the mouth. As with the patch, the idea is to taper the amount of gum you chew over time, until you no longer need it.

Nicotine gum comes in 2 milligram (mg) and 4 mg strengths. The original gum has a peppery flavour that can take some time to get used to. However, the gum is now available in a range of flavours. Chew the gum slowly until the flavour becomes strong and then rest it between your cheek and gum. This process is repeated until the gum has no taste left, usually after 30 minutes or more. The number of pieces of gum that you use should gradually reduce over three months.

Nicotine gum is also believed to help reduce weight gain commonly associated with stopping smoking.

The side effects of the gum include a sore mouth and slight irritation of the mouth and throat

When using nicotine gum, take account of the following points:

- ✔ Stop smoking before using nicotine gum so that you don't overdose.

- ✔ Don't have any food or drinks, especially acidic beverages like coffee, tea, or fruit juice, for at least 15 minutes before chewing, during chewing, and about 15 minutes after chewing. If you do, you may reduce the gum's effectiveness.

Chew the gum correctly to get the benefit from it. You must follow the correct chewing procedure to ensure that the nicotine is absorbed into the bloodstream through the lining of your mouth. Make sure you read the instructions carefully.

- ✔ Keep in mind that you're chewing to avoid or reduce nicotine withdrawal. If you aren't experiencing withdrawal symptoms, you don't need to chew at that moment.

The up side of nicotine gum is that you have more control over the amount of nicotine you take in. You can chew the gum on a regular schedule or chew it only when you feel you need it. Typically, one or two pieces every hour or two do the trick.

Don't smoke while using NRTs as you could suffer unpleasant nicotine overdose symptoms.

Keep nicotine gum out of the reach of children!

Giving nicotine lozenges a try

Nicotine lozenges work in the same way as nicotine gum (see preceding section), delivering discrete amounts of nicotine as you consume them. You use the lozenges for up to 12 weeks, on a tapering schedule. Check the package for the recommended maximum daily dose.

The lozenges come in 2 mg and 4 mg strengths. One way to determine the right dosage for you is to consider the length of time between when you wake and when you have your first cigarette of the day. If you normally smoke immediately upon rising then you need to get your blood level of nicotine right back up after a night's sleep (a night's worth of withdrawal from nicotine). If your smoking is more episodic and less predictable, you may be able to use a lower dose.

If you use nicotine lozenges, be sure to keep them out of reach of children.

As with nicotine gum, allow the lozenge to do its job. Keep it in your mouth for at least 20 minutes. Don't chew or swallow it. Rest the lozenge between the side of your mouth and teeth, as you do with the gum. The lozenge works best when you avoid drinking or eating immediately before and after use.

There is concern that children can mistake these lozenges for sweets, so use caution if you bring this product into a home where children are present.

Succumbing to a microbtab

Similar to a lozenge but much smaller, a microtab contains 2 mg of nicotine and is put under the tongue so that it dissolves into the bloodstream through the lining of your mouth. The number of tabs you take is dependent upon your reliance on nicotine, but no more than 40 should be used a day. Check the recommendations from the manufacturer.

The initial recommended dose when you stop smoking is one or two tabs every hour. The use of the microtab depends on the depth of your addiction to nicotine, but you should not take more than the packet tells you. After up to three months, you should be able to cut down as your psychological need for a cigarette declines. Reduce the number of microtabs you take until you are down to one or two tablets a day, after which you can stop completely.

Microtabs must be dissolved under the tongue. Do not chew or swallow these tabs, as this is likely to cause side effects, including indigestion and stomach and throat irritation.

Talking It Over with Your Doc: Prescription-Only Options

Deciding which type of NRT or drug therapy to use to help you stop smoking is a purely personal decision.

While some people may want to try over-the-counter NRTs, others may like to discuss their options with their GP or a quit-smoking support line before they decide on the best option.

Checking with your doctor about your decision to stop smoking and how you plan to do it is always a good idea. Your doctor may have suggestions or advice based on your health status. For example, if you have had a heart attack then a doctor could offer advice about your options. Your doctor can also offer valuable input on the use and choice of an NRT (especially because some therapies require a doctor's prescription) and can make you aware of potential interactions between nicotine, Zyban, Champix, and other medications you may be taking.

Considering nicotine inhalers

A nicotine inhaler is like other kinds of inhalers in that it has a mouthpiece that pumps single aerosol doses of the product – in this case, nicotine – to the lining of the mouth. The mucous membrane of the mouth and throat is loaded with capillaries and easily absorbs the medication.

The inhaler can be used up to 16 times a day initially, but after two to three months, use should be reduced. You are not recommended to use the inhaler for more than six months.

Comparisons of the inhaler and the patch show them to be about equally effective in promoting smoking cessation. However, one of the psychological advantages of the inhaler is that it approximates the feel of a cigarette because it's an object that you pick up and place between your lips. Not only do you get nicotine, but you simulate, to a certain extent, the action of picking up a cigarette.

Using nicotine nasal spray

Nicotine nasal spray is a handy, highly accessible nicotine delivery system and the strongest NRT available, making it suitable for heavy smokers. Once the nicotine encounters the delicate mucous membranes of the nose, it is absorbed very rapidly. If you use the spray as intended, you can gradually reduce your daily nicotine intake without developing uncomfortable nicotine withdrawal symptoms. Spray users report satisfaction with this product because it provides an almost instantaneous fix for cravings and other manifestations of nicotine withdrawal.

Initially, you can use one squirt per nostril per hour. You use the spray for about three months; two months after starting, reduce the dosage on a daily decreasing schedule. Refer to the package insert for the manufacturer's details on reducing the dose.

Some people develop a nicotine nasal spray habit. It should not be used for longer than six months. Side effects can include sore throat, coughing, sneezing, nasal congestion, weeping eyes, and irritation of the nose. If you have nasal or respiratory problems such as nasal polyps, sinusitis, allergies, or asthma, consult your doctor about using a different nicotine delivery system.

Trying out anti-craving medication

Zyban (bupropion) is an atypical antidepressant that's been used to treat depression and anxiety for a number of years. When used to treat these mood disorders, it usually takes two to four weeks to begin working. The drug is termed *atypical* because, unlike many other antidepressants, it does not seem to act on brain levels of serotonin. Instead, it may boost brain levels of dopamine.

Dopamine, a neurotransmitter, has been implicated in the brain's reward system. It is, broadly speaking, a feel-good molecule. Scientists believe that euphoria, such as that following a good workout or the use of certain drugs, is related to increased activity of dopamine in the brain.

Although some people have concerns about taking an antidepressant to reduce or prevent cigarette cravings, Zyban has been shown to have a fairly specific effect on nicotine cravings. Even if you aren't depressed, Zyban can curb your appetite for cigarettes.

Zyban is not nicotine, so its beneficial effect in countering tobacco addiction works by an alternative mechanism. Zyban works by changing the way you think and feel about smoking. It works directly on the brain, boosting two chemicals that make you feel happier and release feelings of enjoyment. It also reduces the severity of withdrawal symptoms.

Although most people do not experience side effects from this medication, some may notice headaches, jitteriness, or insomnia. Zyban is better taken in the daytime, before bedtime, to avoid the possibility of disrupting sleep. Zyban is not habit-forming and can be stopped at any point without withdrawal symptoms occurring.

Consult with your doctor if you're taking any additional medication, because Zyban has potential interactions with some drugs. Overall, though, it's quite safe.

Champix (varenicline tartrate) is a prescription-only medication available from your GP or the NHS Stop Smoking Service. Similar to Zyban (it is another non-nicotine product), Champix works on the receptors in the brain, stimulating them in the same way that nicotine does, while blocking the effects of nicotine. So you don't get the enjoyable effects of a cigarette or the withdrawal symptoms. Clever, huh? Champix is thought to be more successful than Zyban.

You start Champix before you stop smoking; in fact you have to preset a stop-smoking date 8–14 days ahead. You then take Champix once a day at a low dose for about a week. After that, you increase the strength and take it twice a day. As with other medication, you must read the manufacturer's instructions. You normally take Champix for about three months to complete the course.

Common side effects of Champix include nausea and sleep problems. If you decide to take Champix, you will also be offered motivational support from the NHS stop-smoking services offering encouragement and support to all you folks giving up smoking.

Combining Quitting Aids

Combining quitting aids is the cutting edge of 'quit technology'. Today you have all these tools at your disposal, *plus* nicotine replacement therapies like the patch and nicotine gum, *plus* Zyban and Champix for your cravings (provided that your doctor thinks it's a good idea for you to take this type of medication). Combining quitting aids is where it's at.

If you use a nicotine replacement therapy, you provide yourself with a gradual reduction of nicotine, eliminating nicotine withdrawal symptoms. You need to talk over your options with your health professional, GP, or support counsellor before deciding which aids to combine. This will ensure you do not overdose on nicotine.

Don't forget the support groups also on offer. QUIT, the UK charity, helps smokers stop and can provide details of a specialised clinic or support group in your area. (For details, phone 0800 002 200 or visit the Web site at www.quit.org.uk.) The NHS Stop Smoking Service also provides a variety of support methods, so check it out and use all the help you can get. (Phone the helpline on 0800 1690 169 or visit the Web site at www.gosmokefree.co.uk.)

Chapter 6

Tapping in to the Power of the Mind

In This Chapter

▶ Capitalising on your mind's ability

▶ Exploring hypnosis

▶ Going deep: meditation and health

▶ Exercising without tears

▶ Trying out methods like acupuncture and hypnosis

*A*lternative methods for stopping smoking can complement the more traditional therapies, such as going cold turkey and using nicotine replacement. (For more on those strategies, see Chapter 5.) Combining methods can boost the effectiveness of each one, giving you maximum quitting power. For example, you can use support groups, the nicotine patch, and hypnotherapy. This chapter explains how to go about it.

Some of the methods described in this chapter are not covered by some health insurance plans. Check with your insurer to find out what your particular plan does and doesn't cover.

Using Your Mind to Help You Stop Smoking

Did you know you have an incredible tool at your disposal to help you stop smoking? One that, if you harness it correctly, can turn quitting smoking into the most positive and healthiest thing you can ever do for yourself in your lifetime?

Never underestimate the power of your mind. It works in ways that scientists are still trying to fathom out. But what they do know is how the brain reacts chemically to different situations and what happens when we tamper with it through drugs. (See Chapter 2 for more on the effects of nicotine on your brain.) You can choose to use your mind in a positive, health-enriching manner if you choose.

There are several different approaches to using your mind to help you stop smoking. Changing the way you view smoking on an emotional and physical level lies at the heart of such change. Cognitive behavioural therapy for example, concentrates on the way people think and act to help them overcome behavioural problems, especially those that are unhealthy, like smoking. Hypnotherapy uses techniques to relax the mind and open it to suggestibility.

If you want to know more about these techniques then *Cognitive Behavioural Therapy For Dummies* by Rob Willson and Rhena Branch (Wiley) and *Hypnotherapy For Dummies* by Mike Bryant and Peter Mabbutt (Wiley) may be of interest to you.

You don't have to try and change your mind about smoking on your own. Therapists, hypnotherapists, and support group leaders are all trained to help you deal with change. Call upon all the support you can to make those changes positive and life-enhancing for you.

Figuring Out What Hypnosis Is All About

You may have thought about trying hypnosis, or hypnotherapy, in your effort to rid yourself of smoking.

Scientists struggle to understand what happens during and after hypnosis. All we know is that for some people, it works and helps them stop smoking. Even those who have successfully used hypnosis have different ideas about their state of mind before, during and after hypnosis. However, it is thought that hypnosis can change what is stored in the unconscious mind, especially habits and, as smoking is a habit, it follows that hypnotherapy can have a positive impact on this awful habit. The important fact to remember is that hypnotherapy doesn't just help you quit, but it also helps you remain a non-smoker.

The temptation to look for a pill, a treatment, or a hypnotic suggestion that will forever rid you of the scourge of cigarettes is understandable. Most people look longingly at the prospect of a quick fix, whether it relates to getting rid of a toxic relationship, money troubles, or health problems. The idea that a magic bullet or elixir can wipe out the problem that's been hounding you all these years is tempting indeed. So it's easy to understand the appeal of hypnosis.

Many people try hypnosis in their effort to stop smoking, and many of them consider it to be very successful in helping them to achieve this aim. Hypnotherapists will tell you that it's not just the stopping smoking that they focus on, but staying stopped that is important. For many would-be quitters, the fear of what happens after they stop smoking is the biggest challenge they face. Hypnotherapy helps the person to prepare and deal with those unknown fears.

Of course, everyone is different and what works for one may not work for another. You may know someone who tried hypnotherapy but didn't find it helpful, while another may have only needed one session of hypnotherapy to stop smoking. It doesn't matter; what does matter is that in your effort to stop smoking you may need to combine a few methods to win the war. For example, you may decide to use counselling, hypnotherapy, and a nicotine patch. It's simply a case of using the tools available to you to your best advantage.

Using hypnotherapy to stop smoking relies on building up your willpower. You must really want to stop smoking to get the best from your hypnotherapy sessions and make them work for you.

Contemplating Meditation

Another form of hypnosis to consider is self-hypnosis, which is a form of meditation. It's yet another way to achieve a state of quiet and calm.

Self-hypnosis and meditation have so much in common that, to keep it simple, we refer to both practices as meditation.

So what exactly is meditation?

Meditation can be almost anything. There are many types of meditation – practically as many types as there are personalities walking this planet. You can meditate at work, while watching your child play, or while walking your dog. You can be consumed by meditation while tending your garden. In order to use meditation to stop smoking, the most suitable is the kind that can be done anywhere.

There is no single formula for meditation or for stopping smoking. Try different approaches and use the ones that works best for you.

Think about the idea of 'need'. What do you need? Do you really need a cigarette? Do you need another pair of shoes? (Maybe you do!) Do you need a Maserati? As you get increasingly in touch with your feelings and with yourself, you may come to a whole new understanding of what you *really* need.

As a smoker, you already know how to hypnotise yourself. In fact, you already *have* hypnotised yourself. Each time you light up, you go into a trance. You are, in a manner of speaking, acting out a post-hypnotic suggestion: 'You will light up a cigarette even though everything in the world tells you that it's a bad idea.' You go into a trance-like state in which you turn off your regular concerns about your body, your health, and your future.

When you inhale, you achieve a state of mind that's relaxing and alerting at the same time. This is the sought-after quality of nicotine.

The good news is that you can reach an identical state of mind by self-hypnosis or meditation. When you get really proficient at meditation, you may become able to turn off all thoughts and feelings at will, even the thought, 'I'm not thinking anything!' Once you've cleared your mental field, you can go almost anywhere you want. Remember, as with any kind of exercise, the more patient you are the better you get at it.

When it comes to meditation, practise makes perfect. Within a week, you can reach a state of mind that is quite inspiring.

Appreciating and controlling your breathing

Breath is the vital current of life. You've probably heard this so often before that it sounds like a cliché. 'Don't smoke' is a cliché, too. But facts of life that you ordinarily take for granted, such as your body, your breath, and your heartbeat, can become powerful allies or irritating reminders of mortality and limitation.

A great place to start with breathing is to appreciate it simply and directly. Although breathing is a miracle of the body's construction when it works well – which it usually does when you don't tamper with it – it can wreak havoc when it goes awry. If you've ever had a bout of the flu or, worse still, pneumonia, you'll understand. A persistent cough and a problem with the air supply to your body and brain is no laughing matter. (See your doctor if you have a persistent cough.)

Meditation involves breath control, relaxation, and a state of 'floating'. While you meditate, the goal is to be aware of your body but not of your surroundings. You are aware of your body and breathing, and then slowly but surely you become unaware of your body and breathing. A great deal of evidence suggests that breath control, mind control, and the serenity that they lead to results in healthful changes in your cardiovascular and immune systems.

Breath control is the opposite of smoking. With the breath control that you achieve through meditation, you take back control over your body.

Meditation and breath control is not a touchy-feely thing. Although it requires sitting still, it's physically challenging.

Hundreds of terrific books, tapes, and Web sites are devoted to the subject. For example, see *Meditation For Dummies,* by Dean Ornish and Stephan Bodian (Wiley).

Changing the Way You Think

Sometimes, what we need to do is change the way we think, but that's usually easier said than done. Neuro-linguistic programming (NLP) does just that. With the aid of qualified practitioners, this modern form of psychotherapy works on the principle of encouraging you to change and adapt your thinking so that you can break free from negative thoughts, allowing you to vary your behaviour to achieve the results you desire.

How does neuro-linguistic programming work with stopping smoking? By changing the way you think about smoking and the pleasures it gives you and taking away the fears associated with withdrawal symptoms. Through NLP, many people have successfully quit. Many would-be non-smokers fail at the first hurdle because they are so daunted by the withdrawal symptoms they believe they may suffer that they can't stop smoking to find out for themselves if they will suffer them! Such is the power of the mind.

Not everyone experiences withdrawal symptoms in the same way.

See *Neuro-linguistic Programming For Dummies,* by Romilla Ready and Kate Burton (Wiley), for more information on this technique.

Cognitive behavioural therapy is yet another mind tool in the battle to stop smoking. This therapy offers mental techniques to enhance your motivation and desire to stop smoking, boosting your confidence and self-esteem and helping you deal with the aftermath of stopping. How, you might ask? By changing your thoughts and, therefore, the way you feel about certain aspects of your life. You see, it's not just the stopping you need to worry about; it's the staying stopped. (See Chapter 8 for further details of cognitive behavioural therapy.)

Maximising Your Motivation

To enhance your chances of stopping smoking, you need to be fired up and ready and willing for the challenges that lay ahead of you. Thinking about stopping smoking in a positive manner is a start, just as having a plan for when you are tempted or likely to relapse is important. You have to find all the inspiring reasons for giving up smoking and apply them. So write a list of all the desires and dreams that you think you can and will achieve when you give up smoking. Remember though that taking action is motivating. Don't keep thinking about what you want – take action now!

Surround yourself with positive people, those who are encouraging – you know the types we mean. The ones who say 'You can do it and you will do it' not those who add 'Yes, but . . .' Retrain your mind through the processes available to you, so that negative thoughts are thrown out and positive affirmations fill your brain. Sure, everyone has a bad day, a low day or simply a down day, but it doesn't have to be like that every day, and it doesn't have to stop you achieving your wishes, goals, or ambitions.

Motivation is the key to enjoying everything you do and to wanting to continue.

Stopping smoking requires you to rethink all your old thoughts about smoking and the pleasures it brings. You need to find all the reasons why you want to stop and embrace them with a passion and a desire to clean up your act, your health, and create a new you without cigarettes. Take advantage of understanding how to change your thoughts and be motivated by using the power of your mind. If you need help to do it then use a therapist trained in mind-changing techniques to guide you.

Exorcising Nicotine with Exercise

Believe it or not, physical exercise is a form of medication. It's a way of boosting your wellbeing in a dependable, consistent, and healthy fashion. Vigorous exercise, the kind that gets your pulse pounding and your body sweating, is good for you (unless you have a medical condition that limits the amount and/or kind of exercise you can tolerate. Check with your doctor first.). Exercise feels good. The right kinds of exercise kick off *endorphins* in the brain, which give you the feel-good factor.

Stopping smoking can be a double blessing for you. Not only are you getting rid of a life-depriving and financially costly habit, but you're also launching yourself in the direction of a number of awesome new possibilities. Which of the following activities have you dreamed of doing but couldn't because of limited stamina or lung power?

- ✔ Jogging
- ✔ Running a marathon
- ✔ Climbing a mountain
- ✔ White-water rafting
- ✔ Riding a bike
- ✔ Sailing
- ✔ Playing tennis
- ✔ Playing football

You may be one of those fortunate people who are able to work out despite the fact that they smoke. But don't let this fool you into thinking that you can have it all. Once you stop smoking, your capacity to exercise and the enjoyment you get from it will increase exponentially.

If you struggle with exercise, then why don't you try QUIT's Keep Fit series of exercises (check out their Web site, www.quit.org.uk/programme.htm for more information). It's an exercise programme that has been specifically designed for smokers who want to stop. There are four levels of intensity to cater for a wide range of fitness abilities.

Choosing the best exercise for you

Exercise comes in many forms, so don't be overwhelmed or set your expectations too high if you haven't exercised in along time. Simply becoming more active on a daily basis is a good way to start. Brisk walking for at least 30 minutes every day will help clear your mind and make you feel better. Simple changes such as cycling to work, parking the car further away from your destination, or getting off the bus one stop earlier are all a start.

Find a way to achieve fitness that doesn't make you grit your teeth. It needs to be fun! Try dancing classes – great fun, social, and a really good form of exercise. Or how about joining a running group? Running groups offer all kinds of jogging and running advice and support for people from beginners to the more experienced. You could save the money you would usually spend on cigarettes and use it to buy personal training sessions, gym membership, or maybe a stationary bike – there is no excuse for not cycling and watching TV! If that's not your thing, how about swimming or taking up a physical exercise class? Whatever you decide, you need to do it regularly to get the best from it. Not only will it make you feel good, but you will also look better and tone up.

Exercise is a healthy way to achieve focused wellbeing. You're sure to find the kind of exercise that achieves this state of being for you if you try hard enough.

Trying Acupuncture

Acupuncture, a 2,000-year-old system of Chinese medicine, is based on a theory that the body's energy flows in meridians. *Meridians* are considered to be the natural channels through which the body's energy flows.

Acupuncturists treat a variety of disorders by accurately placing needles to stimulate these critical energy points. The treatments often need to be done regularly and can be costly if you have them carried out privately.

Alternative or complementary approaches such as acupuncture can be used with nicotine replacement therapy (see Chapter 5), counselling, and sheer determination to quit. If you decide to try acupuncture, make sure that the practitioner is certified.

Chapter 7

Staying Smoke Free

· ·

In This Chapter

▶ Preparing to stop

▶ Identifying relapse triggers

▶ Handling self-blame and guilt

▶ Avoiding second-hand smoke

· ·

*A*t some point in your battle against smoking, you suffer a defeat. Just when you think you're doing so well and accomplishing so much, you have a relapse. You give in and have that cigarette after dinner. You're feeling guilty, weak, and angry with yourself for giving in.

Relapses are common, and the important thing is not to use this relapse as an excuse to give up and stop quitting. In this chapter, you find out what to do when you have a relapse, how to handle cravings, and how to deal with other smokers as you're trying to stop.

Planning a Strategy for Success

Stopping smoking takes not only the right mindset but also the right body set and environment set. In other words, not only do you need to be thinking, 'Yes, I can do this,' but you also need to prepare your body for the change and make adjustments to your surroundings to give yourself the best possible chances of success.

What do you need to do as you prepare to take the leap that may save your life? As you contemplate what being without your old friend will be like, visualise what you will need as you approach your stopping day. You may find it helps to write down your thoughts and actions on a piece of paper, so you can see what you need to plan for.

Here are a few ways that you can make sure you don't relapse:

✔ After you choose a specific stopping date (see Chapter 4), make sure you are ready for it – you'll be surprised how quickly it will come round. It's no use, for example, arranging to visit friends who smoke on the day you have chosen to give up!

✔ Gleaning the wisdom you gain from this book and from your conversations with others who have given up smoking, work out a specific strategy. Include exercise to help lessen tobacco cravings. Regular exercise – particularly aerobic exercise, which gets you breathing faster and increases your heart rate – releases endorphins, which make you feel better. Consider adding regular workouts to your stopping plan.

✔ Ask yourself whether there are other ways to help you feel healthier and fitter? Eating the right foods will go a long way towards this goal. Your body responds more positively to a mix of proteins and fruit and vegetable carbohydrates than it does to fat-laden fast foods. Eating properly gives you more energy (which is something you may have relied on cigarettes for).

You don't have to gain weight when you stop smoking. Chapter 8 gives more advice on this subject. Change the way you think about smoking. Neuro-linguistic programming and cognitive behavioural therapy offer practical mental approaches to making positive life changes.

✔ Don't forget to harness the power of your mind (see Chapter 6).

✔ Minimise your exposure to other people's tobacco smoke. Fortunately, the new smoking laws that went into effect in 2007 offer you a chance to work and socialise away from harmful second-hand smoke and help improve your chances of success.

✔ Get rid of all your smoking paraphernalia – lighters, ashtrays, and matches. Clean your car ashtray and make sure you get rid of the smell!

✔ Make a detailed plan for week one and schedule in all the activities you intend to do to ensure you don't reach for a cigarette. Fill in Table 7-1 to ensure you plan thoroughly and help deflect and prepare for any relapses.

Table 7-1	Quit Plan, Week 1			
	Exercise	Activity	Food	Entertainment	Nicotine Replacement Therapy
Quit day 1				
Quit day 2				
Quit day 3				
Quit day 4				
Quit day 5				
Quit day 6				
Quit day 7				

Finding a Quitting Buddy

A quitting buddy is yet another form of support – a social and emotional tool that can help make the difference between a lukewarm effort and a resounding success. You're more likely to succeed if you team up with someone who's in the process of stopping or who has already quit and can be there for you throughout your effort to kick the habit.

You can learn from others' failures as well as from their successes. An essential ingredient of quitting success is learning what *not* to do.

You may find someone close to home – a family member or a colleague – who will team up with you. But if you prefer someone more distant, plenty of Web sites can hook you up with faraway quitting buddies through online chat groups.

The important thing is to find a quitting buddy whom you feel truly supports you.

Sticking with Stopping

Relapses are wakeup calls, not swan songs. Surrendering to the impulse to smoke can be disastrous if it leads to renewed smoking. However, relapses can be opportunities to find out more about your triggers and how to handle them better the next time around. But obviously you don't want to have a relapse in the first place if you can help it.

Relapse prevention is the most important ingredient for letting go of cigarettes. More people are stopping smoking than ever before. Former smokers know more about handling cravings, recognising triggers, and substituting healthy habits for nicotine. Systematic research demonstrates the positive impact of prevention efforts on smoking behaviour. As you go through these strategies for staying clean, try them out and see which ones work for you.

More is better. The more skills and healthy habits you acquire, the lower your chances of a relapse.

Assessing your relapse risk

The first step to practising early relapse prevention is to find out how close you are to relapsing. Identifying your risk for relapse and avoiding high-risk situations can help you on your journey to recovery.

Your risk for relapse is on the rise when you:

✔ Have just recently stopped.

✔ Feel so confident that 'just one more can't hurt'.

✔ Buy a pack 'just in case'.

✔ Don't discard that last pack.

✔ Expose yourself to people, places, and things formerly associated with smoking.

✔ Hang out with friends who smoke.

✔ Are in high-stress situations that usually lead to a smoke, such as family conflict, deadlines, or social obligations.

✔ Are in low-stress situations, such as on holiday, that invariably lead to smoking because you want to maximise your relaxation.

If you can relate to any of these points, you're at risk of relapsing into the habit.

Watching out for common relapse triggers

Relapse readiness is the opposite of stopping readiness. Does that sound confusing? Actually, it's quite simple. Basically, your risk of relapsing to smoking may be triggered by any number of rationalisations that you use to let yourself off the hook, so that you can slip back into the habit.

Smokers who relapse, generally share some common rationalisations, some of which may be very familiar to you. Even if you haven't caught yourself rationalising yet, watch out for these pitfalls anyway! Even the mighty have fallen as a result of buying into these illogical messages. If you're aware of the following rationalisations, you can practise early prevention and stop yourself from getting back into the smoking habit:

✔ 'Despite all my resolutions, I just smoked. I'll never do it again.'

✔ 'Just one more won't make a difference. The damage to my health is already done.'

✔ 'There's no need to stop right now. I can always start afresh tomorrow (or next week or next year).'

- ✔ 'Everyone else smokes and they look fine. I'm in great shape, and I have plenty of time before I need to stop.'

- ✔ 'I'm dealing with so many other problems that I just can't take this one on right now.'

- ✔ 'I worked/played hard and earned this cigarette. I deserve a break.'

- ✔ 'Low-tar/low-nicotine cigarettes are not as danger-ous as regular ones.'

- ✔ 'If I don't inhale deeply, my lungs won't be dam-aged.'

- ✔ 'I simply don't care. I'm going to smoke.'

- ✔ 'I broke my vow by smoking this morning. There's no point in trying to get back on track now.'

Fortunately, you can use self-talk to combat these ratio-nalisations, as described in the next section.

Staying on track

Anyone who has tried to stop smoking has rationalisa-tions by the dozen. (For more on these common triggers, see the preceding section.) If you've just recommitted to abstinence ('I'll never do it again!'), good for you! This book is filled with tips on what to do, where to go, and who to contact in order to stay smoke-free. (If you need help, see Chapter 12 to find ten sources of support.)

When you find yourself making the following excuses, take heed of the real facts which follow:

Picking up: Cycling from rationalisation to relapse

Most people prefer to think of themselves as unique, as people whose behaviour is spontaneous, interesting, and perhaps even creative. The sequence of relapse behaviour, on the other hand, is as predictable as the sun rising tomorrow.

Wannabe quitters light up after buying into one or more rationalisations or after getting exposed to a compelling *trigger* (anything that reminds them of smoking). The pleasure and utter familiarity of those first puffs are tainted by a cascade of guilt and self-blame. You may think, 'Oops, I did it again,' or, 'I'm pathetic, I have no control over myself,' or, 'I'm a slave to my habit.' These feelings of helplessness and self-loathing earn compound interest. The more you've tried to stop, the worse you feel about each subsequent failure.

If you're not smoking right now, you're succeeding. This breath is the first fresh one of the rest of your life. It doesn't matter how many times you've failed in the past. Most successful quitters have three or more quit attempts behind them.

✔ **'One more cigarette won't hurt me.'** The fact is that each additional cigarette does make a difference. Every additional puff increases your exposure to tobacco's toxic effects. The damage to your health is cumulative. Even if you smoked earlier in the day, a walk outside, a drive, a shower, or a glass of juice is way better for you than that next cigarette. Don't say that it's too late to stop, that the damage is already done. Not true! The damage to your health from smoking is always cumulative. The more and longer you smoke, the more grievous the effect on your body. Fewer cigarettes are better than more. And none is best of all.

✔ **'I can start afresh tomorrow.'** Well, like they say, the road to hell is paved with good intentions. You should have your recovery planned out from hour to hour; don't put your health and lung liberation on hold. Accumulated tomorrows add up to *never.* Turn to Chapter 3 right now.

✔ **'I look and feel great.'** Appearances can be deceiving, as can the rationalisation that other smokers look fine. Although the smoker in the jogging suit looks to be in the pink of health, you have no idea what a chest X-ray may reveal. Nor are you there in the morning when gobs of bronchitic phlegm are being hawked up.

✔ **'I'm too busy to tackle that now.'** Sure, you have a lot on your plate. If you feel that you have so many problems that you cannot take on staying smoke-free right now, take a paper and pen and list those problems. Assign each problem a number. Which problem takes priority? Is your current and future health somewhere at the bottom of the list? Is it possible that stopping smoking may actually empower you to master some of the other challenges you face?

✔ **'I deserve a break.'** Of course you do, but don't reward yourself by giving in and having a cigarette. When you give up a compelling habit like smoking, you need to substitute other gratifications. You need to have other goodies to look forward to. What if you went shopping or cooked a great meal or had a massage next time you really wanted a smoke? Find health-promoting ways to please yourself.

- ✔ **'It's just a low-tar/low-nicotine cigarette.'** Thinking that low-tar or low-nicotine cigarettes are okay is one of the more dangerous rationalisations. In fact, low-tar and low-nicotine cigarettes are every bit as dangerous as the normal ones, because people who switch to them end up smoking more and inhaling more deeply. Try carrot sticks, other fresh vegetables, sugarless gum, and lots of liquids instead.

- ✔ **'I don't inhale . . . really.'** Inhaling less? Though you think that inhaling less won't damage your lungs as much, you still need to think about mouth, tongue, and throat diseases that result from exposure to tobacco and tobacco smoke.

- ✔ **'I don't care about my health.'** Many smokers claim that they don't care about their health because they don't care about their future, but is this really true? How many things do you do each day that are geared towards the future? Each of these actions demonstrates that you're planning on being here tomorrow. Take the money you would have spent on cigarettes today and set it aside for a future treat.

- ✔ **'I already blew it today, so I may as well have another one.'** Lose that perfectionism! Just because you broke your non-smoking vow doesn't mean that it's all over. All-or-nothing thinking gets you right back to where you don't want to go. Are you so harsh on yourself in any other areas of your life? Why be this way about an issue that ultimately is so important?

Feeling guilty for relapsing into smoking is a powerful trigger too. Don't be a self-blaming relapser. Understanding what caused the slip is different from beating yourself up over it. Don't surrender to these negative feelings. When you're feeling low, any of the rationalisations 'I'll never be able to stop,' 'What difference does it make if I smoke?' 'I have no self-control anyway,' and the classic 'I'm a loser' may kick in and cause you to pick up the habit again.

Handling Relapses

One struggling smoker said, 'Stopping? No problem. I've done it a thousand times.' Sound familiar? Losing momentum, losing hold of your best intentions to stop, and losing control is what relapse is all about.

The effort to stop is a life-and-death battle for your health, your dignity, and your future. If you're fully committed to this struggle, if stopping is your number-one priority, then this is war!

Here are some steps you can take to win the war:

- ✔ If you do light up, practise immediate damage control. Don't finish the cigarette (and certainly, don't finish the pack!). Limit the amount of physical and psychological exposure you have to the smoke.

Get into the habit immediately after a relapse of turning towards other (non-smoking) activities. Get out of the house. Take a walk. Call a friend. Go to the gym. Take a shower. Put as much distance between yourself and that cigarette as possible.

- ✔ Place a lot of psychological distance between yourself and the relapse. Don't fall prey to self-condemnation, self-blame, and self-pity. As you have seen, these negative states are potent relapse triggers themselves. Do try to understand what led to the lapse, try to avoid setting up similar situations in the future, and continually remind yourself that you're succeeding if you're not smoking right now.

✔ Think positive. Relapsed smokers face many temptations. Think of these temptations as fire-breathing dragons. They're big, they're scary . . . and they're figments of your imagination. Don't make a mountain out of a molehill, for example by convincing yourself that you'll never stop because you've slipped.

✔ Don't start feeling guilty and depressed if you have a relapse. Remember, millions of people just like you have managed to get beyond relapses too.

✔ If you've lit up after deciding to stop, view the experience as a slip rather than a fully-fledged disaster. If you surrender to feelings of disaster, you're more likely to throw up your hands in disgust and say, 'The heck with it, I may as well smoke.'

Lighting up doesn't mean giving up. All it means is that, on this particular day, at this particular time, you lit up. That's it. (Not the end of the story.) A small defeat doesn't have to lead to even larger failures. Each tobacco-free moment is a fresh and healthy start. Each cigarette-free day is another victory. An accumulation of smoke-free moments, days, and eventually weeks is what makes for success.

If you do have a cigarette:

✔ You're not a bad person.

✔ All your intentions, choices, and decisions are not spineless or ineffective.

✔ You can still succeed at quitting.

Do whatever it takes to immediately start reaccumulating good, healthy stopping time. Throw away whatever cigarettes remain. You can lose the battle and still win the war!

Staying focused

Your success at staying clean hinges on your ability to remain focused on the task. Stopping smoking is not a casual project. It's not a hobby. The decision to stop is a decision to make abstention from cigarettes the main priority in your life until it is no longer a problem.

Typically, the first few days or weeks following smoking cessation are a difficult time. Newly abstinent smokers are bombarded with distractions, temptations, nicotine craving, episodic bursts of energy (and valleys of fatigue), anxiety, insomnia, and even depression. You may face some, all, or none of these difficulties.

Holiday time, especially around Christmas and the New Year, may be the wrong time for you to stop smoking. This time of year abounds with triggers and motivators to light up. On the other hand, you may be one of those people who are truly and highly motivated by New Year's resolutions. Go for it! Just make sure that you think about when is the best time for you to stop.

The challenge is to stay on target. With the aid of right thinking, exercise, plenty of liquids, and perhaps nicotine replacement therapies such as the patch (see Chapter 5), you'll be equipped to handle even the most unpleasant of rides, provided that you're committed to seeing the process through.

Stay focused. Think of yourself as you want to be: free of a habit that has and will continue to drag you down. Remember your first puff ever, and how sick it made you feel? Ever smoked too much? Can you recall feeling your stomach tied up in knots, your head pounding, and your resolution at the time to never smoke again? Those feelings were real. You've made a decision for health – a decision to take the high road. Remaining focused is what will keep you where you need to be.

Reframing relapse: A day without nicotine is a successful day!

Rome, as they say, wasn't built in a day. Neither is healthy cigarette-free living. Freeing yourself from the shackles of smoke is a laborious, time-consuming process that requires a more or less steady input of energy and resolve over an extended period of time.

The path towards liberating your lungs is usually not a smooth one, although many have been able to simply stop and never pick up another cigarette again. More typically, most smokers attempting to stop have periods of success (abstention) interrupted often erratically and unpredictably by relapses.

Relapses are par for the course. If despite your best intentions you surrender to the impulse to smoke, your next move must be to exert immediate damage control. It's much better to smoke one cigarette and then fire up your renewed resolve, jump back on the wagon, and pick up exactly where you left off.

What you don't want to do is use the slip as an excuse, a kind of flabby justification, for a full-blown relapse. The rationalisation may take the form of 'Well, that proves it. I just can't stop, so I may as well go ahead and have as many as I want.'

Wrong. Dead wrong. The less you smoke and the sooner you reclaim your intention to stop forever, the better you feel. Not only will your throat and lungs and cardiovascular system feel immediately better, but so will your self-esteem and dignity. You'll probably enjoy a heightened sense of self-confidence, of empowerment. You were tempted, were swayed momentarily by an errant impulse, gave in, and then got right back on track.

Another thing: Many, if not most, smokers who are just starting out can have a fair amount of physical and emotional discomfort, especially during the first several days of not smoking. Some new quitters complain of pervasive tiredness, lethargy, and an inability to focus or concentrate. Others feel wound up. Newly abstinent ex-smokers often feel that they're miserable and useless and can't get anything accomplished. Their minds are in a blur.

That's fine. A day without cigarettes is a successful day, regardless of how little or how much you accomplished, provided your number-one priority for now is stopping smoking. The investment now in time and energy, even if it means reduced productivity or fatigue, is going to pay off in major ways in the near future. You'll have excess energy and drive and will further benefit from eliminating all the distraction and time and expense that went into getting smoking supplies and taking the innumerable smoke 'breaks' that interrupt so many smokers' work and home lives and recreation.

Your effort to stop is aided by numerous resources, such as support groups, quit lines, exercise, nicotine replacement therapies and Zyban. (See Chapter 5 for more.)

Keep in mind that the path you're on has been trodden by millions of others before you. Stopping smoking, though not easy, is possible. It's a reachable goal that you can achieve.

Handling Second-Hand Smoke When You're a Quitter

Second-hand smoke (smoke that is passively inhaled from others' cigarettes) has become a major public health issue – so important that the Government introduced the smoking ban to stop non-smokers having to suffer the effects of second-hand smoke in social and work environments.

Second-hand smoke is toxic and may result in physical injury and illness. As many as 50,000 people are estimated to die each year as a result of second-hand smoke.

If your spouse, partner, or room-mate is a smoker, you face extra challenges as you stop smoking. Maybe they don't want to alter their lifestyle to accommodate yours?

If this is an issue with your family and friends then you need to talk to them about it. Many partners and family members of quitting smokers are willing to go all the way to facilitate their loved ones' success, even to the point of stopping themselves. Perhaps you can agree compromises that are helpful, such as not leaving cigarette packs around the house or only smoking outside the house or car.

A related issue is that of foetal exposure to nicotine and the hundreds of other chemical compounds in cigarette smoke. The intrauterine environment offers no alternatives, unlike second-hand smoke situations where you may be able to avoid further contact and inhalation of smoke. Whilst you can remove yourself from the effects of a smoker, the developing foetus doesn't have a choice.

Developing Cognitive Skills for Success

You have a powerful set of tools at your disposal to succeed at stopping. One is this book. Another is your body, which responds to your careful and loving attention by feeling better and giving you the green light for your continued and greater efforts to live healthily, eat properly, exercise, and breathe clean air.

Your social network – including supportive family, friends, colleagues, and your doctor – should be ready to help you as much as necessary. (If you want their support, you need to tell them what you're doing.) Don't forget the NHS smoking helpline or the charity QUIT, which provide tailor-made support to suit you (check out Chapter 12 for contact information for these organisations).

Last, but certainly not least, is your mind. Your mind is your greatest ally in your effort to stop – so great, in fact, that we dedicate Chapter 6 to this topic. Laying the mental and emotional foundations for success involves frequent reminders to yourself in a positive way.

Cognitive behavioural therapy is a school of healing that trains people to identify thoughts and feelings that may contribute to depression, anxiety, and negativity. Hypnotherapy has also proved very successful for helping people to stop smoking.

Once you've stopped, invoke these ideas as often as necessary:

✔ I may feel shaky or tired or miserable today, but what I'm going through is temporary. The situation will get better every day.

✔ Even if I don't feel great, I'm having a successful day because I'm not smoking.

✔ Stopping smoking is a loving, caring thing to do for myself. I deserve it.

✔ I don't have to surrender to the impulse to smoke. I can do something else instead. I will feel much better about myself tomorrow knowing that I didn't slip.

Part III

Looking at Special Groups

In this part . . .

In this part we examine the complex relationship between moods and cravings for cigarettes. Mood dips and swings are usually fleeting, and your decision to quit smoking can outlast moment-to-moment emotional fluctuations. You may also be concerned about the possibility of putting on weight when you quit. Weight gain is not an inevitable consequence of quitting smoking; on the contrary, your health and physical appearance are likely to improve when you stop smoking.

Pregnant women need to be aware of the specific impact that tobacco products have on their growth and development and on the growth and development of a baby. In this part we talk about those effects and give you information about helping a pregnant woman give up smoking.

Chapter 8

Smoking, Depression, and Weight Gain

In This Chapter

▶ Understanding depression

▶ Axing anxiety

▶ Weighing in on weight control

▶ Exorcising tobacco, not exercise

*T*his chapter describes mood and anxiety problems that may cause you to reach for a smoke, and the link between weight gain and stopping smoking. Understanding the varieties of mood disorders is important because they occur more frequently among smokers than among non-smokers. (We also help you recognise that you don't have to get fat when you stop smoking!)

There are far better and healthier solutions to emotional highs and lows than lighting up.

What Is Depression?

Depression has to be one of the most commonly bandied-about words in the English language. The term (when it's not referring to the economy) refers to a gamut of different mood and feeling states. When people speak of depression, they may be referring to any or all of the following:

- ✔ Stress
- ✔ Moodiness
- ✔ Irritability
- ✔ Low energy
- ✔ Loss of interest or pleasure
- ✔ Low self-esteem
- ✔ Difficulty concentrating
- ✔ Agitation
- ✔ Anxiety

In recent decades, psychiatrists and other mental health professionals have made giant strides towards a better understanding and characterisation of depression.

Depression is one of the most common disorders in the UK. Although it's very treatable, it needlessly accounts for a great deal of suffering and debility. If you think you're depressed, please see your GP.

Depression is a complicated matter and usually goes on for a long period. Depression is characterised not only by negative moods, thoughts, and behaviour, but also by physical changes such as sleeping problems, crying, and irregular eating habits. It makes coping with everyday life difficult, and while everyone can get a little 'down', the symptoms of depression do not go away, affecting work and relationships.

Alleviating Anxiety

Anxiety often accompanies depression and vice versa. Like depression, anxiety has many other names, such as stress, 'nerves', and agitation.

Anxiety is an ordinary part of life. Flipping through this month's stack of bills can be quite stressful. So can crossing the street! But there are limits to how much anxiety is normal. As with depression, the signal that you should consult a professional is when the anxiety interferes with your life.

Anxiety is the inner or subjective counterpart of a perceived danger. The key word here is *perceived*. Your body and brain are hard-wired to react instantly and effectively to danger signals around you. Imagine that you're crossing the street and suddenly, seemingly out of nowhere, an articulated lorry comes bearing down on you: the classic fight-or-flight situation. Your muscles tense, your heart pounds, you hyperventilate. Inside your body, adrenaline and cortisol prepare you to react swiftly and effectively. Your pupils widen to maximise your awareness of the environment. Bear in mind that all this happens on a scale that is way out of proportion to any real danger in your environment.

People with anxiety disorders have continuous bouts of fight-or-flight reactions. The causes of these responses are multiple. Some people inherit a tendency towards anxiety or panic. For others, catastrophic, violent life events trigger the anxiety.

If you've ever had anxiety symptoms, you'll be quick to recognise these features:

✔ Dry mouth

✔ Sweaty palms

✔ Racing pulse

✔ Quick, shallow breathing

✔ Intense sense of foreboding and impending doom

Even when they're transient, anxiety symptoms are extremely unpleasant. Perhaps you've had the occasion to speak in public and found your stomach tied up in knots, your thoughts confused, and your heart racing. This is called *performance anxiety.* A related experience, *social anxiety*, occurs when you are in a crowd, at a party or meeting, for example. In these situations, your nervous system may go on overload and pump out stress hormones as though your life were truly on the line. Knowing this, it's no wonder that nicotine, with its anti-anxiety effects, is so difficult to kick!

The problem (aside from the extreme unpleasantness of the sensations) is that ongoing stress reactions are damaging to your health. Studies have shown that unchecked stress responses, including anxiety, essentially wear down the immune system and thus make you more susceptible to infections.

Smokers 'self-medicate' anxiety, including panic attacks, when they experience a sudden overwhelming fear without any apparent reason or warning, with cigarettes. Although small amounts of nicotine act as a stimulant, greater amounts exert a sedative effect. The sight of a harried, stressed-out person reaching for a smoke is so familiar that it has become a cliché. Also, because nicotine is a stimulant, it can actually provoke greater anxiety and further panic attacks.

Although very frightening, panic attacks are not dangerous. They are most common between the ages of 15 and 25, but can develop at any age.

If you want to explore in more detail how you can deal with anxiety, check out *Overcoming Anxiety For Dummies*, by Elaine Iljon Foreman, Charles H. Elliot, and Laura L. Smith (Wiley).

The principle of drug karma

Do you smoke to stave off or reduce anxious feelings? If you have recognisable anxiety, the answer to this question is likely to be 'Yes'. But you need to know that all drugs that affect the brain cause rebound – whatever goes up has to come down, and whatever goes down has to come up.

Anxiety under the microscope

Extreme anxiety is the equivalent of a fire alarm going off in your brain. The *locus ceruleus,* a tiny brain centre with intimate connections to the rest of your nervous system, fires off the neurotransmitter *norepinephrine* in what are, relatively speaking, huge amounts. This sudden flood of norepinephrine turns on all kinds of other warning systems in the brain and in the rest of the body, resulting in physiological bells and whistles and the urgent message to all body systems: 'Fight or flight!'

Consider another sedative, alcohol. The first drink or two makes you feel relaxed and helps you unwind. You may feel more comfortable and sociable around people after you've had a drink. Several hours later, however, the picture is quite different. Instead of feeling loose and relaxed, you may begin to feel uptight. Your nerves may be on edge. If you've had too much to drink and fallen asleep, you may wake a few hours later feeling wired and anxious.

This is your brain going into rebound. Once the alcohol – the sedative – has been metabolised and is out of your system, your brain overreaches in the opposite direction like a spring that has been compressed and then released.

The principle of drug karma applies to stimulants such as nicotine as well. After some minutes of increased energy, alertness, and excitement, the only direction to go is down. Following the nicotine rush (which you notice especially when you have your first cigarette of the day or when you abstain from smoking for several hours and then light up), you experience a physical letdown. You're tired; probably more fatigued and played out than before you had the cigarette.

Don't despair. You can do plenty of things, many of them on your own, to combat anxiety, as the following section explains.

When you do cut back and eventually completely cut out cigarettes, you may have a temporary increase, or rebound, of anxiety symptoms. To get through rebound (nicotine withdrawal) anxiety:

✔ Remember that the anxiety is only temporary.

✔ Engage in physical activity such as walking or jogging.

✔ Consult your doctor if the anxiety is severe enough to interfere with your functioning.

✔ Keep a log of your wellbeing. Chances are, over the course of the first week you stop smoking, you will see a dramatic reduction in the amount of rebound anxiety you experience.

Cognitive behavioural therapy

Cognitive behavioural therapy may be helpful for mild to moderate anxiety and depression. It's based on the idea that beliefs determine feelings. The things you tell yourself throughout the course of the day create and then reinforce how you end up feeling and functioning.

For example, a depressed person tends to be pessimistic. If you're depressed, you're likely to interpret events, even neutral events such as the weather, in negative ways. A depressed person wakes up to an overcast sky and reads it as proof that his life and future are dark and will always be that way. It's possible, even likely, that these interpretations (of which dozens, if not hundreds, occur in the span of a day) trigger emotional and even physical reactions that are ultimately destructive.

The first step in cognitive behavioural therapy involves identifying the self-statements that you make all the time. The next step involves singling out the negative, irrational statements and holding them up to the light of day. For example, is your belief that you will never be able to stop smoking really true? If you think about it, haven't literally millions of others been able to stop? What is it about yourself that you think will stand in your way?

After that, it's a case of replacing your negative thoughts with more logical, constructive beliefs. For example, you may believe that you can't, or never will, stop smoking. When you examine this belief, you may be able to reframe it in a more positive way, such as, 'I used to think I couldn't stop. Millions of people have quit. I probably can, too.'

For more information on cognitive behavioural therapy, check out Chapter 6. If you want to get an even firmer grasp of the subject, try *Cognitive Behavioural Therapy For Dummies*, by Rhena Branch and Rob Willson.

The Truth about Quitting Smoking and Weight Gain

Smoking and eating are intimately related. For starters, many, if not most, smokers smoke after meals!

Smoking after a meal has become a social and biological reflex. The cigarette-after-meal connection may relate to the fact that nicotine acts as a stimulant. After taking a meal, particularly a large meal or a meal accompanied by alcoholic drinks, people like to perk themselves up with a smoke. Part of successful stopping is working out a new behaviour pattern for after meals and every other time you're accustomed to having a smoke. The new smoking laws have helped. Restaurants are no longer places where smokers can light up, making it easier to change that after-meal cigarette habit.

Plenty of smokers actually substitute cigarettes for food. 'Why not?' you might ask. 'Who couldn't stand to skip a meal or two?' Simply reaching for a cigarette instead of sitting down for a meal may seem convenient. These days, most people are so busy that they find themselves reaching for whatever is the fastest cure for those hunger pangs as they rush from work, school, or a family event to the next important meeting. If you could see what smoking does to your body from the point of view of your arterial walls, intestinal lining, and cardiac and lung chambers, though, you would never think that a cigarette is an acceptable substitute for a meal.

You may have a fear (or even an outright horror) of gaining weight, and perhaps you prefer to take on whatever damage the cigarettes are doing. However, stopping smoking and watching your weight at the same time is possible. You don't have to be a movie star to take care of your body inside *and* out.

One technique that dieticians use to help compulsive eaters overcome their problem is to have them record all the foods they consume. The same idea applies to cigarettes. Imagine taking all the cigarettes you consumed in the last six months and laying them out in front of you. You would be stupefied! At least food is either metabolised, eliminated, or stored as fat. The waste products of tobacco combustion are stored in the linings and cells of your throat and lungs – not a good place for toxins!

Remember that you're in charge of what you eat, what you drink, and what you smoke. If you're feeling out of control about eating or smoking, put yourself right back in the driver's seat. As you stop smoking, these after-eating strategies may help you stay away from cigarettes:

✔ Make a phone call.

✔ Get right up and take a walk.

✔ Read to your children.

✔ Walk your dog.

✔ Kiss someone.

✔ Have a mint or a stick of gum.

✔ Go out.

✔ Read a section of this book.

✔ Take a shower.

✔ Take up an activity that involves using your hands, like model-making or sewing.

You have to eat. You don't have to smoke. Don't let a fear of weight gain keep you from putting your health first.

Staying away from fattening quick-fix foods

Although eating foods that are bad for you isn't nearly as bad as smoking, there is a limit! You can find a wealth of information about calorie intake, food groups, the best time of day to eat or not eat, and even the ideal state of mind to be in while taking your meals and snacks. Avoid at all costs fast foods and high-sugar foods such as sweets, cakes, and pastries.

High-fat foods, such as those you get at takeaways and pizza parlours, are the gastrointestinal equivalent of smoking. A burger alone, not including the extras, such as a slab of cheese, can have 20 or more grams of saturated fat. Pizza and similar foods are no bargain if you're watching your weight or your cholesterol.

The best foods to eat, whether it's quit day 1 or quit day 1,000, are high-protein, low-fat, unrefined-carb foods such as chicken, fish, whole grains, and tofu. Wholegrain foods are also high in fibre. Other generally healthy high-fibre foods are vegetables and fruits.

Drink water when you eat food high in fibre, as your body does not digest fibre. Your body needs a little lubrication to move the fibre through your digestive system!

The things of value in this life, such as health, longevity, and continued good looks, don't come easy. You have to work at and invest in them. The good news is that the initial down payment is quite low – a pack of cigarettes. Don't stop there, though. Once you stop smoking, you will want to keep boosting your feelings of wholeness and wellbeing. Lifestyle changes such as eating healthier foods and getting more exercise pay off big time.

Unrefined carbohydrates are slow releasing, providing you with energy throughout the day. Stay away from refined carbohydrates: white bread, crumpets, white rice, and pasta.

Doing your part by exercising regularly

Want a quick weight loss? Then increase your activity levels and literally burn the fat off. It takes commitment and regularity though. Don't think that if you do some exercise today, you can forget about it for the rest of the week. Build up to exercising if it's something new to you or if stiff and sore muscles may put you off. The art is to combine cardiovascular activity with strength work; so jogging, dancing, and cycling are all great for working up a sweat and making the heart work, while working with light weights or machines helps to build your strength and continues to work long after the session. Don't just take our word for it – try it and see!

Regular exercise feels great. No kidding. Find the kind that works for you, and you'll be eager to stick with it.

It doesn't matter whether you join a gym, hire a personal trainer, or slog it out in your lounge. What matters is that you work out regularly.

The kind of workout you choose depends on your preferences. The duration and frequency are more important than the activity itself. If you have health problems or are no longer young, consult your doctor before you begin any exercise regimen.

Finding food substitutes for nicotine

During the fragile transitional days and weeks when you first stop smoking (congratulations!), you may want an oral substitute. Try the following suggestions:

- ✔ **Chewing gum:** Gum, particularly sugarless, may be helpful.

- ✔ **Raw vegetables:** Carrot and celery sticks are great because they are practically calorie-neutral and are extremely portable.

✔ **Chopped fruit:** Good for you as it helps increase your levels of antioxidants, which mop up *free radicals* – highly reactive molecules that damage cell structure. Free radicals are implicated in many diseases, including cancer and heart disease. The toxins from nicotine and cigarette smoke create free radicals. Eating fruit will also increase your vitamin and mineral intake.

Keep a bottle of spring water on hand. It's filling and delicious.

Counting calories, not cancer sticks

Sometimes, obsessing is a good thing. If you're concerned about gaining weight after quitting, why not put your energy to good use and learn as much as you possibly can about nutrition, weight control, and exercise? Focusing your thoughts and efforts in this direction not only distracts you from the desire for a cigarette, but also informs you of the better world that's within your grasp.

Chapter 9

Smoking, Fertility, and Pregnancy

In This Chapter

▶ Finding out about smoking's effects on fertility

▶ Looking at the devastating consequences of maternal smoking on a foetus

▶ Recognising the effects of smoking after pregnancy

*G*etting pregnant, carrying a baby to term, and raising a healthy, loving child are unequalled among life's positive experiences. If you smoke, your habit puts all these things – your ability to conceive, your chances of carrying your baby to term, and your child's health – at risk. This chapter looks at the negative effects of smoking on mother and baby (and on dad, too!). It also provides tips and strategies for supporting a pregnant woman's efforts to quit smoking.

If you're pregnant or thinking about getting pregnant, it is imperative for you to stop smoking. Your health is at stake and so is the health of your baby.

If you're pregnant, you need to discuss any drug you are taking with your doctor. Because nicotine is a drug, it can interact with other drugs you take.

Smoking and Fertility

Cigarette smoking has a significant negative impact on fertility. A variety of toxins from cigarette smoke can impair a person's ability to conceive. And it's not just active smoking that reduces fertility. Exposure to second-hand smoke can have the same result too.

Long-term smoking may result in reduced fertility or fertility problems in both men and women.

- ✔ **Women:** Conception takes longer (more menstrual cycles) for smokers than it does for non-smokers. The more a woman smokes, the more likely fertility (and health) problems will occur.

  Even in very low amounts, cigarette smoking can significantly reduce your ability to become pregnant.

- ✔ **Men:** Compared to non-smokers, men who smoke have fewer sperm. The sperm they do have are less motile than those of non-smoking men, and the chemicals in tobacco smoke may alter the chromosomal makeup of male genetic material. This damage can be passed along to the developing foetus, resulting in a variety of physical abnormalities or even subtle changes in the brain, affecting behaviour that emerges later in life.

Smoking, menopause, and ageing

Smoking causes more than just fertility problems in women:

✔ Women who smoke have up to a four times greater risk of developing cervical cancer than non-smokers do.

✔ 'The change' (menopause) occurs earlier in smokers.

✔ Evidence suggests that long-term smoking causes many of the manifestations of ageing. Smoking may cause wrinkles, for example, and your insides age more rapidly too.

Risks to the foetus

The first three months of pregnancy, known as the first *trimester,* is the most critical period of development for a growing foetus. During the first three months, the organs and tissues are especially vulnerable to toxic and traumatic influences. The last thing a growing foetus needs is a steady supply of poison coming downstream from mum and passing through the placenta and into the foetus. Exposure of the foetus to most drugs, including tobacco, can result in significant or subtle damage to the unborn child, particularly during the first trimester.

Recent research reveals that smoking can have the following physical effects on a growing foetus:

✔ Children of mothers who smoke during the first trimester of pregnancy have a greater chance of being born with a cleft palate.

- ✔ Children of mothers who smoke more than 15 cigarettes a day during pregnancy have more illnesses during their first months of life. Some of these illnesses are serious ones for which the baby may need to be hospitalised.

- ✔ Pregnant women who smoke have almost twice the risk of giving birth to a low-birth-weight baby. Babies who weigh less than 2.5 kilograms at birth face a greater risk of illness and even death during infancy and the toddler years.

- ✔ Babies born at less than 2 kilograms may have an increased likelihood of complications such as cerebral palsy, mental retardation, and behavioural problems.

If you quit smoking during the first trimester, you increase the chance that your baby will be born at a normal birth-weight.

- ✔ Evidence suggests that maternal smoking raises the chance of the baby arriving sooner than expected.

Not smoking during (and after) pregnancy goes a long way towards giving your baby the chance to grow up healthy, smart, and well-adjusted.

Nicotine is very addictive. As few as four cigarettes a day can lead to chronic nicotine addiction. There's no such thing as casual smoking, especially if you're pregnant.

Smoking-related complications

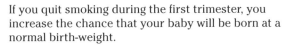

Not only does smoking put the foetus at risk of all sorts of health and mental problems, but it can also put the entire pregnancy and sometimes the mother's life at risk.

Developmental milestones

If you need additional reasons not to smoke while you're pregnant, think about your unborn child in terms of these milestones:

Weeks 9–12: The foetus is 50–80 millimetres (mm) long; nourishment and waste removal takes place through the placenta and umbilical cord.

Week 16: The foetus's face looks distinctly human.

Week 20: The foetus is 24 centimetres (cm) long and weighs 375 grams (g).

Week 26: The foetus's eyes are open.

Week 28: The foetus is 30 cm long and weighs 700 g; the lungs became capable of breathing.

Week 38: The foetus is 45 cm long and weighs about 2.75 kilograms (kg).

Miscarriage, or spontaneous abortion, occurs more frequently among women who smoke. Generally speaking, pregnant smokers have a higher rate of other kinds of problems in pregnancy and delivery as well, including:

- ✔ Bleeding during pregnancy; sometimes severe.

- ✔ Abnormal placement/location of the placenta, which makes delivery difficult and potentially dangerous.

- ✔ Ectopic pregnancy (the embryo starts growing in a site other than the uterus; almost all these pregnancies fail).

Sudden infant death syndrome

Sudden infant death syndrome (SIDS), also known as cot death, is the unanticipated death of a baby who seemed to be in good health. The death remains unexplained even after extensive medical investigation. SIDS, a horrible and tragic event in any family's life, is more common among children of parents who smoke.

The risk of *stillbirth* (the death of an infant within the first hours of life) is significantly increased when the mother smokes. Also, 30 per cent of deaths caused by *sudden infant death syndrome (SIDS)*, known as cot death, could be avoided if parents didn't smoke around their children. (See the sidebar 'Sudden infant death syndrome' for more information.)

If you smoke, now is the perfect time to stop. You have some choice over the kind of air you breathe. Your baby doesn't.

Stopping Smoking During Pregnancy

Smoking during pregnancy puts both the mother's and the baby's health at risk. Stopping now, even if you're already pregnant, lowers the risks to you and your baby.

Possible harm to the foetus seems to relate directly to the amount you smoke. The less you smoke, the better your baby's chances of being born healthy.

Many pregnant smokers have spouses or partners who smoke as well, increasing the temptation to have 'just one' while trying to stop. Most of the women who are able to stop smoking while pregnant pick up again after pregnancy.

Second-hand smoke can also affect foetuses, but the effects depend on much smoke the foetus is exposed to and for how long. For example, a smoking partner increases the chances of a non-smoking mother's baby dying by over three times the chance if she had a non-smoking partner. However, being with a smoker for a few hours will obviously not have the same devastating effects.

You may wonder whether it's okay to use the patch or some other form of nicotine replacement therapy, such as nicotine gum, nicotine aerosol spray, or the nicotine inhaler, during pregnancy. This issue is a complicated one that you should discuss with your doctor. Although these therapies will expose your unborn baby to nicotine, that nicotine may be less harmful than persistent heavy smoking, which exposes the foetus not only to nicotine but to other dangerous chemicals as well. You and your doctor can work out together what is safest for your developing baby.

Tell your doctor if you are depressed or having anxiety or other emotional symptoms and are giving up smoking while pregnant.

Smoking and Breast Feeding

When breast feeding, be aware that any drugs you take, including nicotine and other chemicals in tobacco smoke, are present in your breast milk and are passed along to your baby. Babies who breast feed from mothers who are heavy smokers (20 or more cigarettes a day) can develop nausea, vomiting, stomach problems, and diarrhoea. Also, smoking may affect breast-milk production, which could make it difficult for you to breast feed your baby at all.

For your baby's sake, don't smoke if you breast feed!

The Long-Term Effects of Maternal Smoking

Researchers are discovering all kinds of provocative and scary information about the effects of parental smoking on children's development. For example, sons of mothers who smoke at least ten cigarettes a day during pregnancy are much more likely to develop antisocial personality disorders than sons of non-smoking mothers.

When a pregnant woman smokes, not all the effects of smoking show up right away in the infant. Some of the effects of exposure to toxic compounds, particularly behavioural ones, may appear later in the child's life. Getting pregnant mums to stop smoking is way less expensive than dealing with the multiple, and often devastating, consequences of antisocial disorder later on. Sons of smoking mothers are more likely to become criminals later in life. Evidence suggests that children of mothers who smoke at least 14 cigarettes a day are more likely to develop attention deficit hyperactivity disorder (ADHD).

Medical scientists believe that these problems are due to the decreased oxygen levels reaching the developing foetus. Smoking mothers (and fathers, and, for that matter, everyone) have increased levels of *carboxyhaemoglobin* in their blood. Haemoglobin, which normally carries oxygen from the lungs to nourish the rest of the body, gets saturated with carbon monoxide from cigarette smoke and brings less oxygen to the baby and the mother's body.

Here are some other charming findings:

- ✔ Another large-scale study demonstrated that children of mothers who smoked at least ten cigarettes a day were shorter and scored measurably lower on tests of maths and reading.

- ✔ Infants of parents who smoke are twice as likely to suffer from serious respiratory infections as children of non-smokers. Breathing problems, upper respiratory tract infections, and ear infections are more common for children in smoky environments.

- ✔ The presence of tobacco smoke exacerbates allergies and asthma.

- ✔ Smoking during pregnancy may have implications for a child's long-term physical growth and intellectual development.

- ✔ Evidence suggests that smoking interferes with a woman's hormonal balance during pregnancy, and that this interference may have long-term consequences on the reproductive organs of her children.

- ✔ Listening skills among children whose mothers smoked during pregnancy tested lower.

Part IV
The Part of Tens

'It was a special treat to celebrate
12 months of giving up smoking.'

In this part . . .

*T*his part is made up of quick tips and tools to motivate you to stop smoking for good. You can take comfort in the fact that when it comes to quitting, you're never alone in your decision. Millions of people have been there before. In this part, we look at signs that you want and need to stop, substitutes for smoking, and where to find different forms of support to help you win the war against smoking.

Chapter 10

Ten Signs That You're Ready to Stop

In This Chapter

▶ Knowing when you've reached your smoking limit

▶ Recognising the signals to quit

▶ Fielding others' concerns about smoking

*T*his chapter is a short list of signs that tell you when you're ready to stop smoking. If you survey a large number of people who have quit, you are likely come up with hundreds of signs that made the difference for them in their decision to stop. You may find that it's a combination of several signals that gets you to stop.

You're Developing a Smoker's Cough

Once you start getting regular, persistent reminders that your lungs need a break, and you can no longer write off that cough or congestion to allergies or a cold, you may be ready to quit.

Smoke clogs and contaminates the whole intricate breathing system you were born with. No longer able to do its job, the system becomes more congested, and infection, such as bronchitis, may set in. Pollution in your lungs just lies there in stagnant little pools, inviting infection. You cough, you wheeze, and you spit, but nothing shifts the gunk clinging to your lungs.

A sure sign of bronchitis is the presence of yellow or yellow-green mucus. Consider that mucus a sign that your body is ready to stop. How about the rest of you?

Your Wallet Feels the Crunch

When cigarettes are putting a major hole in your budget, you have a very real, concrete indicator that the time to stop is now. Smoking is hitting you where it hurts – your wallet.

The price of a pack of cigarettes has risen steadily and dramatically over the past several years. Smoking has become an expensive lifestyle choice that replaces 'luxury' items such as food, shelter, and transportation. There's every reason to believe that the cost of cigarettes will continue to rise.

You're Willing to Walk a Mile for a Cigarette

Ever feel that stopping smoking is just too much trouble? All the planning it takes, the self-denial, the self-control, the mental and behavioural strategies you need to employ – why bother?

Dedicated smokers leave no stone unturned when it comes to staying supplied, however. Many hapless smokers have found themselves in desperate need of a smoke at inconvenient times (say, at 2 or 3 a.m.) or in inconvenient places, but even at times like these, no effort is too great to hunt down the elusive weed.

It's time to stop when you go out of your way for a cigarette.

You Feel Like a Social Misfit

Look at them – the people at work who huddle outside buildings in all weather, at all times of day. They have a hunted look, an aura of guilt, of turning the other way when they're seen. Each one clutches a little tube of rolled tobacco. They inhale furtively, greedily, intent on taking in enough nicotine to last them until their next smoke break in two or three hours.

Nicotine is still a mind-altering drug. As society changes its ways, the new smoking laws show that smoking is no longer something others have to put up with.

The point is, each time you smoke around others, you run the risk of being criticised, stigmatised, pitied, and even abhorred.

You're Unable to _____ (Fill in the Blank) without a Smoke

If you're unable to do what you want to do without the need to have a smoke somewhere along the line, the act of smoking has become a habit. After you've become accustomed to lighting up along with a particular activity, the act of smoking becomes a reflex, as in, 'I can't have dinner without having a cigarette afterwards,' or, 'I can't get out of bed in the morning without having my first cigarette of the day.'

Nicotine is highly addictive and therefore fuels this habit. However, you can change your habit, with a lot of willpower and some professional help.

You Feel Guilty

Feeling guilty is a natural emotion for most smokers. You either experience self-hate each time you light up or after you've smoked a cigarette, or you experience self-pity: 'I didn't want to have that cigarette; I really will stop smoking now that I'm pregnant.' Both of these emotions are better known as guilt.

It's bad enough feeling this way about yourself without having someone load guilt on you. This book is not aimed at criticising you. It's meant to be a meaningful resource that you can use at any time, repeatedly, until you don't need it any longer. You'll get plenty of criticism from other sources to intensify your feelings of guilt. If you're like most smokers, you've already had more lectures than you can stand.

Don't underestimate the accumulated impact of these statements on your wellbeing and your self-regard. You probably don't like to be told again and again that you're making bad choices. Quite often, the direct result of being told what to do (or admonished) is to do the opposite.

You Smoke More and Enjoy It Less

Are you finding that you're smoking more and enjoying it less? As with so many other 'pleasures', smoking has a window of maximum enjoyment. Many smokers find that it's all downhill after the first hit of the day. Somehow, the 200 or so puffs that follow the day's first don't compare in taste or impact. The alerting or calming effect of successive cigarettes lessens as the day progresses.

When you consider the downsides – the cough, the acrid taste, the yellow fingers, the ever-mounting health debit that smokers try to ignore – it's understandable that those who smoke more get less and less pleasure out of the activity as time goes by.

You React to Negative Comments

The first dozen or so negative comments from family, friends, and other concerned people may roll off your back, unheard and unheeded. But after a while, these remarks start to become guilt-provoking and bothersome in the extreme.

When you think about it, you are (if you want to be!) accountable not only to yourself but to those you love and care for. The responsibility is enormous. When friends and family members question you about your smoking, part of what's troublesome is that they're showing more concern about your health and future than you are.

Although many people around you will benefit from your quitting, you need to stop primarily for yourself. But one of the many perks of stopping is that not only do you please yourself, but you also end up pleasing plenty of other people at the same time.

You Miss Your Senses of Smell and Taste

Your five senses are a complex and finely tuned instrument capable of detecting minute levels of sensory input. Your smell receptors, located in your nose, are able to differentiate among particles at the molecular level. Your palate is likewise composed of an array of extraordinarily high-tech receptors on the tongue, grouped according to taste type.

You can also lose these senses. Continued exposure to toxic chemicals, such as tar, nicotine, and the other constituents of tobacco, erodes the sense of smell and taste over the course of years. The good news is that after you quit smoking, your sensitivity and receptivity make a comeback. This recovery may seem like a small matter, but once you get a hint of the banquet of fragrances and flavours that you have let slip over the years, you're likely to appreciate them more.

You Want a Healthier Future

Many people live from day to day, or even from moment to moment, rather than plan for the future. How do you see your future? Does it involve a stair lift . . . or a portable oxygen tank? Do you see yourself getting fitter, healthier, more energetic, and more resilient with the passage of time, or becoming increasingly wrinkled, tired, and dependent on tobacco and possibly medications and medical equipment?

To some extent, the choice is yours. Granted, everyone inherits a genetic programme for illness or health (usually a combination of the two). But ultimately, what happens to you is the consequence of *both* inheritance and your environment. You do have some control over your surroundings, your body, and your fate.

Stopping smoking is not just about tossing out the cigarettes; it's also about taking care of that priceless vehicle, your body.

Chapter 11

Ten Great Smoking Substitutes

In This Chapter

▶ Getting in shape physically and mentally

▶ Refocusing your priorities

*Y*ou've probably heard the saying that if you give up a habit, you need to replace it with another habit — preferably a healthy one! Smoking is no different.

If you are to succeed at stopping smoking, if you are to give up a 'friend' that has stuck with you through thick and thin, you need to replace the habit with something else. Substituting alternative rewards and gratifications for cigarettes is a matter of harm reduction: You want to replace the cigarette habit with a habit that is supportable and less harmful than cigarettes – and hopefully not harmful at all. This chapter gives you ten good habits to consider.

Working Out

If you find yourself feeling jittery or stressed as you stop smoking, you may want to give exercise a try. Not only is a workout such as jogging, tennis, or walking good for almost anybody, but it's also a great way to calm your nerves and feel centred, thanks to the *endorphins* (the brain's feel-good molecules) that exercise triggers. You feel healthy, bright, and clean after a good workout.

Exercise comes in many forms. From weight-training to aerobics, yoga, or Tai Chi, the choice is endless and all types of exercise are worthwhile. If you feel you can't venture forth into the gym, consider an activity or sport that you have always wanted to try, or resurrect one you enjoyed from your schooldays. It doesn't matter what you do so long as you get up and do it. For some ideas, check out *Fitness For Dummies,* by Suzanne Schlosberg and Liz Neporent (Wiley).

Commit to get fit and you will physically see the changes to your body as well as experience them mentally.

Having More Time

Time is one of the most precious commodities around. Everyone complains that the day doesn't have enough time in it and fantasises at one point or another about having more time. So what would you do with an extra five hours of free, uncommitted time a week?

Chances are, if you've given up smoking, you do have that extra time. Think about it. How much time did you spend each week purchasing and then smoking cigarettes? Five or ten hours? What did you have to show for that time? Now's the time to acknowledge that you can do something useful with those extra hours.

Drinking Lots of Fluids

Drinking lots of fluids actually supports your attempt to quit. Increased amounts of fluids literally help wash out some of the toxins and pollutants that have accumulated in your body as a result of using tobacco.

Drinking water helps to flush out toxins from the body and keeps you hydrated. Being dehydrated is often mistaken for hunger.

Have a glass of freshly squeezed orange juice every day. Some evidence suggests that cigarettes burn up ascorbic acid, or vitamin C, in the body, and Vitamin C from orange juice is a great way of putting it back.

Meditating

Meditation is one of the most powerful and gratifying tools available to you. The beauty of meditation is that it's easy to learn and extremely portable. You can meditate anywhere and at almost any time. When you first start to meditate, you may grow impatient and distracted with the process, but remember the more you practise the easier it will become – a bit like smoking really!

For more information about meditation, see *Meditation For Dummies,* by Dean Ornish and Stephan Bodian (Wiley).

Reaping the Power of Positive Thinking

Focusing your mental energy, your perceptions, and your immediate responses to the world outwards is a great strategy for success at stopping smoking and for success in general.

Changing the way you think about smoking and your attitude towards it will help you understand the habit you developed and the changes you need to make to ensure you stay smoke free. Cognitive behavioural therapy and neuro-linguistic programming are methods that work on changing your negative thoughts to positive ones and improving your confidence and your emotional and mental thinking. These ideas have been used by many successful people to develop their working and personal lives.

 These strategies are unbelievably effective and help not only with stopping smoking, but with many other personal challenges as well. For more information on the power of positive thinking, see *Neuro-Linguistic Programming For Dummies,* by Romilla Ready and Kate Burton (Wiley), or *Cognitive Behavioural Therapy For Dummies,* by Rob Willson and Rhena Branch (Wiley).

Using Nicotine Replacement Therapies

Chapter 5 gives you the scoop on everything you need to know about nicotine replacement therapies. We mention them in this chapter for two reasons:

✔ We want to remind you of the wealth of tobacco alternatives and substitutes that exist.

✔ Life and the things that arouse your excitement and curiosity are the real nicotine replacement therapies. People are nicotine replacement therapy. Work and creation are nicotine replacement therapy. After all, what is therapy? It's any activity that promotes health and healing.

Getting Five a Day

Eating fruit and vegetables may not sound very exciting, but they are packed full of antioxidants that help mop up the free radicals racing through your body. Smoke from cigarettes pollutes your body, causing thousands of free radicals to be released throughout your system. Consequently, your ability to absorb vitamins and minerals is compromised, causing premature ageing and ill health. At the same time, smoking also lowers the antioxidants in your body, so stopping smoking and eating at least five fruits and vegetables a day helps to redress the imbalance.

So, not only are you putting back something healthy into your body, but you are also eating foods that won't make you put on weight. Get two for the price of one!

Visualising Health

Visualisation is quite interesting. It's a double-edged sword. On the one hand, it's important to appreciate the impact that seeing things the way you want them to be has on your life and feelings. On the other hand, it's also important not to blame yourself inappropriately for the bad things that come your way. In other words, visualisation is powerful – but not all-powerful.

If you visualise a life without cigarettes – and I mean visualise in every sense including how you'll look and feel, how food and air and the inside of your mouth will taste, and how an autumn breeze will smell – this continual effort will boost your intention to the point where you're taking more and more opportunities to think about things other than cigarettes.

Visualisation is the step between desire and actualisation. When you deeply and creatively imagine something to the point where you can almost feel, taste, and hold it, it's practically yours.

Changing Your Routine

As a smoker, you have specific routines. When and where to have a cigarette – with a cup of coffee, after a meal or sex, and when you get in or out of your car – are well-worn rituals that have probably become ingrained into your life.

You have to change your routines. And that's not to say it's easy – it isn't – but you have to recognise that smoking has become a habit and it needs to be replaced by another. You can do it. Six weeks is what it takes to make a habit, so aim for six and see what you've replaced a cigarette with by then. If your new habit is not enough to satisfy you, find another habit.

Change your habits.

Getting a Piggy Bank

One thing you will instantly notice about stopping smoking is how much more money you have in your pocket. Don't waste it; make it work for you. Get a good old-fashioned piggy bank and every time you think about a cigarette but don't smoke one, commit to putting a coin in the bank. Or work out how many times a week you would have bought a packet of fags, and put the money saved in the pig. The rewards will be huge. It's your choice whether you want to share them or not!

Chapter 12

Ten Sources of Support

. . . .

In This Chapter

▶ Finding ways to get the help you need

▶ Adapting support to suit you

. . . .

*W*e all know that you may need to get some help along the way to stopping smoking. That support can come in a variety of unusual ways, so take whatever is on offer that you believe will make the difference to turn you from a smoker into a non-smoker.

Buy This Book for You and Your Smoking Friends

Suggesting that you buy more copies of this book sounds like we want the royalties! It's true, but nonetheless, purchasing additional copies of this book and giving them to your smoking friends as gifts is a far better way to go than buying another pack of cigarettes. Face it – you can purchase this book for not that much more than the price of a packet of cigarettes.

If all your friends and family try to stop smoking, you have your own continual self-help group!

Not only that, but think of it as the healthiest present you've ever bought. And the environment benefits!

Use the Internet

You can find literally hundreds of stopping smoking programmes on the Internet. Many have support groups or chat sites attached. While you may not need a different programme to the ones described here, having access to someone online may be useful.

Take Advantage of Group Support

The NHS Stop Smoking Service offers group support sessions in your area. Call it free on 0800 169 0 169 or visit www.gosmokefree.co.uk, text GIVEUP and your full postcode to 88088, or go and see your GP or local pharmacy for further details and help.

Alternatively, QUIT, the UK charity whose aim is to save lives by helping smokers stop, can be contacted at www.quit.org.uk or by phone on 0800 002 200, or text SMOKE to 65151.

One of the main strategies for stopping means having support systems in place for when the going gets tough. Don't give up giving up.

Talk to Your Family and Friends

Sounds simple enough doesn't it? All the people around you will surely help you stop smoking. Well a few may not! If your partner is still smoking, for example, he or she may think life would be a lot easier if you carried on. Or maybe the friend that you meet each week at a certain time for a certain thing, such as a drink, likes nothing more than a cigarette when you socialise. Changing your habits may mean making others around you look at theirs.

So, what do you do about it? Well, be honest for a start. Tell your family and friends that you are stopping smoking and you'd appreciate their help. If they do smoke then maybe they can do it when you're not around and remove all their smoking paraphernalia whenever you are about. Get your friends to understand how much you want to give up, and ask them not to smoke around you.

Use the smoking laws to help you. Meet friends and family in places where smoking is banned.

Call a Counsellor

Chances are that the time when you really need to talk to someone will be at the most unusual time of the day or night. While relatives, friends, and family may complain about a late-night call, specialised cessation counsellors are on hand 24 hours a day to listen and advise.

Try the QUIT charity helpline on 0800 002 200 or the NHS Stop Smoking Service on 0800 1690 169. They may be just the help you need to make it through.

Volunteer

'Volunteer at what?' you may ask. Just about anything really. The more you do for others, be it adults, children, wildlife, or the environment, the more people you come into contact with. Telling them you have given up smoking will mean extra support around you, and you'd be surprised at how many people you may meet who have given up smoking before you. They're usually great sources of support.

Volunteering in and around the community will make you more aware of your surroundings and also, with any luck, your health, especially if you help out with those less fortunate than yourself. Helping at a local hospital or hospice with people who have respiratory problems will open your eyes to the danger you put yourself under by smoking. The experience may be just the thing you need to realise how close you came and how fortunate you are.

Join a Health Club

Research shows that doing exercise when you stop smoking increases your chances of staying a non-smoker.

If you don't already work out at a gym or club, you may have reservations about starting. Part of the reluctance to give it a try may be the expense. However, many facilities are willing to let potential new members have a trial workout or pay for the use of the club one day at a time. Take advantage of those free trials to find a place where you feel comfortable.

Some people, particularly if they're overweight or self-conscious about their appearance, are hesitant to go into a health club where seemingly perfect specimens in Lycra effortlessly crunch hundreds of pounds. But not all health clubs are like that.

Everyone starts somewhere. Even the Greek god striking poses before the gym mirror started out weak, flabby, and insecure.

If you're really shaky about showing up at the gym, visit during an off-peak time of day or night. Many facilities are large enough that you can find a corner or niche where you feel reasonably comfortable and secluded and avoid prying eyes.

If, for whatever reason, you really don't want to join a health club, you can take the money you save on cigarettes and invest in a treadmill or a set of weights, which you can probably set up at home without much difficulty. Having your own equipment gives you virtually unlimited access to exercise without leaving the house.

Working out is one of the best things you can do for yourself. Strenuous exercise, particularly aerobic exercise, is good for your heart, your lungs, your circulation, your muscles, and your head. Exercise can be addictive. It's an addiction you can be proud to have.

Just hours after you have given up smoking, your health starts to clean up its act.

Hire a Personal Trainer

Wouldn't it be great if you could rent a personal quitting trainer?! Well, although that may be a thing of the future, hiring a personal fitness trainer to help you achieve your goals is a possibility. A personal trainer will not only help you to get your body back in shape, but can also help you to feel good, sharpen your mind, and improve your well-being. The benefits of a personal trainer will soon become apparent when you see the results and feel them too. A personal trainer helps you choose your goals in a way that assures that you reach them.

Fitness takes many forms, and what works best for someone else may not be to your liking at all. If you prefer yoga or more spiritually focused activities such as meditation, then look around for classes or join a club where these activities are part of your membership.

Make the Smoking Laws Work for You

New laws, introduced in England in July 2007, make it illegal to smoke in enclosed public places and workplaces. You can make these laws work for you. Designed to help protect the public from the harmful effects of second-hand smoke, these new laws will also help smokers stop.

Make sure your employer abides by the rules! If you can't smoke at work then make sure you don't. Don't be tempted to join those that congregate outside the building for a cigarette. Instead, challenge someone who you would normally join for a cigarette and a smoke to give up too.

If you are the employer then set an example! Display the no smoking signs with pride and introduce some new distractions for all those staff who want to give up.

Failure to comply with the smoke-free law is a criminal offence and can result in a fine.

Socialising in places where smoking is banned is much easier to do now. If you meet friends who do smoke, pick a venue of your choice where they have to follow suit and join you in the ban. If they don't like it, pick new friends!

Write a Blog

Stopping smoking means letting go of a time-consuming habit that you may not have realised meant quite so much to you. Focusing that energy elsewhere in a positive manner is what you need to do.

Writing is terribly therapeutic, and writing a blog or diary of your experiences as you go through the quitting process can work on two levels. In one respect, blogging helps you put all your emotions down where you can see them, and that helps you to focus on them.

However, if you do decide to reveal all online, there is also a good chance that you can reach out to others who are going through the same experience. Being in touch with others in the same situation as you provides another support system that you never knew existed.

Index

• *A* •

academic achievement, 139
action potential, 35
acupuncture, 20, 93–94
addiction, cigarette
  benefits of smoking, 24–26
  decision to stop smoking,
    13–16, 144–146
  defined, 26–27
  overview of, 23–24
  power of, 28
  quitting aids, 17–21
  reasons for smoking, 29–30
  severity of, 30
addiction, exercise, 163
addictive personality, 33
ADHD (attention deficit
    hyperactivity disorder),
    138
adrenaline, 44, 46
aerosolised polyaromatic
    hydrocarbon, 69
ageing, early, 133
alcohol
  anxiety medication, 122
  link to smoking, 26
  mental effects of smoking, 47
allergy, 46, 139

alternative therapy, 83. *See
    also specific therapies*
alveoli, 39
aneurysm, 42
antidepressant, 19, 45, 78–79
antisocial personality disorder,
    138
anxiety. *See also* stress
  alcohol use, 122
  brain chemistry, 121
  health effects of, 120
  nicotine replacement
    therapy, 70
  nicotine withdrawal
    symptoms, 122–123
  overview of, 119
  reasons for smoking, 120–121
  smoking effects, 122
  symptoms of, 120
appearance, physical, 104
arteriole, 45
artery, 45
assessment, of relapse,
    100–101
asthma, 39, 139
atheroma, 45
attention deficit hyperactivity
    disorder (ADHD), 138
atypical drug, 78

• *B* •

BAcC (British Acupuncture Council), 20
Baic, Sue (*Nutrition For Dummies*), 31
bar, 13
behaviour
  children with smoking mothers, 138
  of smokers, 36
birth defect, 134
bladder cancer, 43, 46
blame, 105, 106
blogging, 165
blood
  clots, 42
  vessels, 45
blood pressure
  healing process, 49
  health effects of smoking, 42, 44, 45
  NRT precautions, 70
Bodian, Stephan (*Meditation For Dummies*), 89, 153
brain chemistry
  anxiety effects, 121
  effects of smoking, 34–36
  positive thinking, 84
Branch, Rhena (*Cognitive Behavioural Therapy For Dummies*), 84, 124, 154
breast cancer, 58
breast feeding, 137–138

breath
  control, 88–89
  odor, 41
breathing problem
  children of smoking mothers, 139
  decision to stop smoking, 144
  health effects of smoking, 38, 39, 40
British Acupuncture Council (BAcC), 20
British Complementary Medicine Association, 20
bronchi, 39, 41
bronchitis, 39, 144
Bryant, Mike (*Hypnotherapy For Dummies*), 65, 84
buddy, quitting, 99
bupropion, 19, 78
burger, 126–127
Burton, Kate (*Neuro-linguistic Programming For Dummies*), 65, 90, 154

• *C* •

cafe, 13
calendar, 54
calorie counting, 129
cancer. *See also specific types*
  death from, 28, 38, 41
  health effects of smoking, 38, 41
  susceptibility of smokers, 43

carbohydrate, 127
carbon dioxide, 45
carbon monoxide
  body's healing process, 24, 49
  health effects of smoking,
    39–40
carboxyhaemoglobin, 139
carcinogen, 43, 46
cardiovascular system
  exercise, 128
  health effects of smoking,
    42, 45
carrot sticks, 128
catastrophising, 62
celery sticks, 128
cervical cancer, 43, 133
Champix (medication), 19,
    79–80
change, response to, 55, 60–61
chemicals, in tobacco
  gastrointestinal system, 46
  immune system, 45–46
  liver function, 46–47
  nicotine replacement
    therapies, 69
  overview of, 14
  second-hand smoke, 111
  smoke contents, 10, 36, 43
  water intake, 153
chest infection, 38, 46
chewing gum, 32, 128
children
  death of, 42, 136
  developmental problems, 138,
    139

foetal problems, 132–136, 139
  smoking teenagers, 33–34, 58
chronic obstructive pulmonary
    disease (COPD), 39, 48
cigarette smoking/addiction.
    See addiction, cigarette
circulatory system, 48–49
coffee, 74
cognitive behavioural therapy
  alternative rewards, 154
  motivation to stop
    smoking, 90
  overview of, 123
  power of the mind, 84
  relapse strategies, 112–113
  treatment process, 123–124
*Cognitive Behavioural Therapy
    For Dummies* (Willson and
    Branch), 84, 124
cold-turkey method, 56–57
commitment, to smoking
    cessation, 9, 14
confidence, 30, 100
COPD (chronic obstructive
    pulmonary disease),
    39, 48
cot death, 42, 136
cough
  decision to stop smoking,
    143–144
  health effects of smoking, 38,
    44
counsellor, 19, 161

craving, nicotine
  attachment to smoking, 56
  complementary therapies,
    18–19
  planning strategies, 54
criminal behaviour, 138

• *D* •

daily routine
  alternative rewards, 156
  exercise, 93
  planning strategies, 54–55,
    97–98
dancing, 93
death, smoking related
  babies of smoking mothers,
    42, 136
  cancers, 28, 38, 41
  cardiovascular disease, 28, 42
  chronic obstructive
    pulmonary disease, 28, 48
  leading causes of, 28
decision to stop smoking
  cigarette addiction, 13–16
  commitment, 9, 14
  date to stop smoking, 53–54,
    96
  importance of, 10, 11
  life goal inventory, 11–12
  mental focus, 108–109
  planning tips, 53–54, 95–98
  rationale for stopping, 10
  readiness to quit, 16, 143–149
dehydration, 153

Denby, Nigel (*Nutrition For
    Dummies*), 31
dental problem, 38, 42
dependence. *See* addiction,
    cigarette
depression
  cognitive behavioural
    therapy, 123
  medication, 45
  overview of, 118–119
developmental milestones
  childhood health, 138, 139
  foetal health, 135
diabetes, 42, 70
diary, 165
diet
  calorie counting, 129
  exercise, 127–128
  health clubs, 163
  health effects of smoking, 42
  nicotine gum, 74
  nutrition, 31, 126–127
  oral substitutes for nicotine,
    128–129
  reasons for smoking, 31–32,
    124–125
  relapse, 64
  techniques, 125–126
disease. *See also specific
    diseases*
  fruit benefits, 129
  power of addiction, 28
  smoking-related diseases,
    38–41
dizziness, 70

dopamine
  antidepressants, 78–79
  brain chemistry, 36
  smoking addiction, 27

• *E* •

ectopic pregnancy, 135
Elliot, Charles H (*Overcoming Anxiety For Dummies*), 121
emotion. *See also specific emotions*
  attachment to smoking, 54–56
  pre-contemplator stage, 61
  reasons for smoking, 30
emphysema, 39
endorphin, 91, 152
energy, physical, 63–64
enjoyment, smoking, 147
exercise
  alternative rewards, 152
  benefits, 91
  options for, 92, 162–163
  personal trainers, 164
  planning strategies, 96
  post-relapse activities, 106
  selection, 93
  stress-relief strategies, 32
  support system, 162–163
  weight control, 127–128

• *F* •

factory smoke, 13
failure to stop smoking. *See* relapse, smoking

family
  negative comments from, 147–148
  smoking during pregnancy, 111, 137
  support of, 159, 161
fatigue, 63–64
fattening food, 126–127
fertility, 132
fibre, 127
fight-or-flight response, 119, 121
financial issues, 61, 144, 157
fingernail colour, 41
Fitness For Dummies (Schlosberg and Neporent), 152
focus, mental, 108–109
foetus, 132–136, 139
Foreman, Elaine Iljon (*Overcoming Anxiety For Dummies*), 121
free radical, 47, 69, 129
friend
  negative comments from, 147–148
  quitting buddy, 99
  relapse strategies, 100
  smoking during pregnancy, 111
  support of, 159, 161
fruit
  alternative rewards, 155
  juice, 74, 153
  oral substitutes, 129

• G •

gastric lining, 46
gingivitis, 38, 42
goal setting, 59
guilt
  decision to stop smoking, 146
  feelings related to relapse, 61,
      62, 105
  post-relapse activities, 107
gum
  chewing, 32, 128
  nicotine, 18, 73–75

• H •

habit, substitute, 59–60, 104
haemoglobin, 139
healing process, 48–49
health club, 162–163
health risks
  decision to stop smoking,
      148–149
  NRT precautions, 70
  pregnant women, 111–112,
      132–139
  rationalisations, 103–104, 105
  relapse, 63
  respiratory system, 38–40
  smoking-related diseases,
      38–41, 44–48
  stress reactions, 120
heart attack, 42, 43, 70

heart rate, 44, 49
high blood pressure
  health effects of smoking, 42,
      44, 45
  NRT precautions, 70
hoarseness, 38
holiday, 108
hormonal balance, 139
hypnotherapy
  defined, 84
  NRT complementary
      therapies, 20
  overview of, 64–65, 85
  quick fix versus long-term
      solution, 85–86
  willpower, 86
Hypnotherapy For Dummies
      (Bryant and Mabbutt),
      65, 84

• I •

ICM (Institute For
      Complementary
      Medicine), 20
identity development, 34
illegal drugs, 23–24, 29
immune system
  body's healing process, 49
  health effects of smoking,
      45–46
  stress effects, 120

infant health
  breast feeding, 137–138
  cot death, 42, 136
  foetal health, 132–136, 139
infection, 38, 46
inhaler, nicotine, 18, 77
inhaling smoke, 105
Institute For Complementary
    Medicine (ICM), 20
Internet support groups, 160

• _K_ •

kidney cancer, 43

• _L_ •

laryngeal cancer, 38, 43
law, smoking
  smoke-free zones, 12, 13, 97
  support strategies, 164–165
leukaemia, 43
life goals inventory, 11–12
life span, 27
liquid intake, 32, 127, 153
listening skills, 139
liver, 46–47
locus ceruleus, 121
loss, feelings of, 55–56
low-birth-weight baby, 134
low-tar cigarette, 105
lozenge, nicotine, 18, 75–76
lung cancer, 38, 43, 49

lymphatic system, 49
lymphocyte, 46

• _M_ •

Mabbutt, Peter (_Hypnotherapy
    For Dummies_), 65, 84
macrophage, 45
medication. _See also specific
    medications_
  anxiety treatment, 121–122
  depression treatment, 45
  liver function, 47
  pregnancy, 132
meditation
  alternative rewards, 153
  breath control, 88–89
  defined, 86–88
Meditation For Dummies
    (Ornish and Bodian), 89,
    153
men, 132
menopause, 133
mental attachment, 56
mental focus, 108–109
meridian, 93
microtab, 76
mind, power of, 84–85, 97, 112
miscarriage, 135
mood disorder. _See specific
    disorders_
motivational strategies, 90–91
mouth irritation, 74
mucosa, 46

• N •

nasal spray, nicotine, 18, 78
nausea, 44, 70
Neporent, Liz (*Fitness For Dummies*), 152
nervous system, 34–36
neuro-linguistic programming
  alternative rewards, 154
  overview of, 65, 89–90
Neuro-linguistic Programming For Dummies (Ready and Burton), 65, 90
neuron, 34–35
neuroreceptor, 36
neurotransmitter, 35, 36, 121
New Year's resolution, 108
NHS Smoking Helpline, 19
NHS Stop Smoking Service, 81, 160
nicotine
  body's healing process, 49
  cravings, 18–19
  effects on body, 27, 34–36
  food substitutes, 128–129
  versus other drugs of abuse, 23–24, 29
  overdose of, 70, 72
  stress link, 120–121
  tobacco-alcohol link, 26
  withdrawal symptoms, 17
nicotine polacrilex, 73
nicotine replacement therapy (NRT)
  alternative rewards, 154–155
  combination therapies, 80–81

complementary therapies, 19–20
defined, 17
function of, 68–69
over-the-counter options, 17–19, 70–76
overview of, 67
precautions, 68, 69–70
pregnancy, 137
prescription options, 17–19, 76–80
support groups, 81
nicotine withdrawal
  anxiety, 122–123
  challenges to stopping smoking, 15–16
  cold-turkey method, 57
  described, 17, 68
  function of NRTs, 68–69
  positive thinking, 89–90
  pre-contemplator stage, 60
  quitting aids, 17–20
  relapse, 63–64
  types of, 15, 44–45
norepinephrine, 121
NRT. *See* nicotine replacement therapy
nutrition
  oral substitutes for nicotine, 128–129
  planning strategies, 96–97
  weight control, 31, 126–127
Nutrition For Dummies (Denby, Baic, and Rinzler), 31

• *0* •

odor, breath, 41
oesophageal cancer, 43
office, smoke-free, 13
online support group, 160
oral cancer, 43
oral contraceptive, 42
oral fixation, 128–129
orange juice, 153
Ornish, Dean (*Meditation For Dummies*), 89, 153
osteoporosis, 42
Overcoming Anxiety For Dummies (Foreman, Elliot, and Smith), 121
overdose, nicotine, 70
oxygen, 39–40, 139

• *P* •

panic attack, 121
paraphernalia, smoking, 97, 161
parent, smoking, 33
patch, nicotine
  described, 18, 71
  versus nicotine inhaler, 77
  safety, 71–72
  tips for use, 73
peer pressure, 33, 58
perfectionism, 105
performance anxiety, 120

periodontal disease, 42
personal trainer, 164
phlegm, 48
physical attachment, 55
physical change, 60
piggy bank, 157
pizza, 126–127
positive thinking
  alternative rewards, 154
  motivation strategies, 91
  neuro-linguistic programming, 64–65, 89–90
  planning strategies, 97
  post-relapse activities, 107
  power of, 84
pre-contemplator stage, 60–61
pregnancy. *See also* women
  fertility, 132
  infant health, 132–136
  long-term smoking effects, 138–139
  medication effects, 132
  nicotine replacement therapy, 137
  NRT precautions, 70
  second-hand smoke, 111–112, 137
  smoking spouses, 137
prevention tips, 58
psychotherapy. *See specific types*
public transportation, 13

• Q •

QUIT programme, 20, 81, 92, 160
quitline, 19
quitting aids, 17–21

• R •

rationalising smoking, 101–106
Ready, Romilla (*Neuro-linguistic Programming For Dummies*), 65, 90, 154
relapse, smoking
  common triggers, 101–102
  mental focus, 108–109
  planning strategies, 96–98, 99–100
  post-relapse actions, 106–108
  power of mind, 112–113
  quitter's perspective, 109–111
  quitting buddy, 99
  rationalisations, 101–106
  reasons for, 61–64
  risk assessment, 100–101
relaxing activity, 63, 88, 101
respiratory infection, 139
respiratory system, 38–40
restaurant, 13, 124
reward, for not smoking, 59–60, 151–157
Rinzler, Carol Ann (*Nutrition For Dummies*), 31
ritual, 55
running, 93

• S •

Schlosberg, Suzanne (*Fitness For Dummies*), 152
second-hand smoke
  health effects of smoking, 41
  pregnancy, 111–112
  smoking laws, 97
sedative, 122
self-hypnosis. *See* hypnotherapy; meditation
senses, 148
shop, 13
SIDS (sudden infant death syndrome), 42, 136
skin
  nicotine patch, 72
  wrinkled, 42, 47
sleep, 72
smell, sense of, 148
Smith, Laura L (*Overcoming Anxiety For Dummies*), 121
smoking
  body's healing process, 48–49
  daily routine, 54–55
  emotional attachment to, 54–56
  enjoyment of, 147
  mental health effects, 47–48
  physical health risks, 38–41, 44–48
  reasons for, 27–34, 120–121, 124–125
  smoke contents, 10, 36, 43
  smoke-free zones, 12, 13

smoking, decision to stop
  cigarette addiction, 13–16
  commitment, 9, 14
  date to stop smoking, 53–54, 96
  importance of, 10, 11
  life goal inventory, 11–12
  mental focus, 108–109
  planning tips, 53–54, 95–98
  rationale for stopping, 10
  readiness to quit, 16, 143–149
smoking relapse
  common triggers, 101–102
  mental focus, 108–109
  planning strategies, 96–98, 99–100
  post-relapse actions, 106–108
  power of mind, 112–113
  quitter's perspective, 109–111
  quitting buddy, 99
  rationalisations, 101–106
  reasons for, 61–64
  risk assessment, 100–101
social problem, 120, 138, 145
spouse, 137
stillbirth, 136
stomach cancer, 43
stomach lining, 46
strengthening exercise, 128
stress. *See also* anxiety
  addictive personality, 33
  exercise, 32
  reasons for smoking, 30, 32–33
  smoking relapse, 62, 100
stroke, 42

sudden infant death syndrome (SIDS), 42, 136
support group
  described, 19
  nicotine replacement therapy, 81
  resources, 159–165
synapse, 34–35
synaptic space, 35

• *T* •

taper method, 59
taste, sense of, 148
tea, 74
teenager, 33–34, 58
teeth colour, 42
telephone counselling, 19
thyroid problem, 70
time, having more, 152–153
titration, 47, 69
Together Programme (quitting aid), 20
trigger, 101–102, 103

• *U* •

ulcer, 46
upper respiratory tract infection, 46

• *V* •

varenicline, 19, 79–80
vegetables, 128, 155

visualisation, 155–156
vitamin C, 153
volunteering, 162

• *W* •

walking, 93
water intake, 127, 129, 153
weight control
  calorie counting, 129
  exercise, 127–128
  health clubs, 163
  health effects of smoking, 42
  nicotine gum, 74
  nutrition, 31, 126–127
  oral substitutes for nicotine,
    128–129
  reasons for smoking, 31–32,
    124–125
  relapse, 64
  techniques, 125–126
white blood cell, 45, 46
willpower
  hypnotherapy, 86
  mental focus, 108–109
  relapse, 101–106
Willson, Rob (*Cognitive
    Behavioural Therapy For
    Dummies*), 84, 124, 154
withdrawal symptoms
  anxiety, 122–123
  challenges to stopping
    smoking, 15–16

cold-turkey method, 57
described, 17, 68
function of NRTs, 68–69
positive thinking, 89–90
pre-contemplator stage, 60
quitting aids, 17–20
relapse, 63–64
types of, 15, 44–45
women. *See also* pregnancy
  breast feeding, 137–138
  fertility, 132
  health benefits of stopping
    smoking, 49
  health effects of smoking, 42
  menopause, 133
  NRT precautions, 70
work vehicle, 13
World Health Organization,
    26–27, 41
wrinkled skin, 42, 47
writing, 165

• *Z* •

Zyban (medication)
  described, 19, 78–79
  function of, 45
  safety, 79
  triggers, 64

Notes

······································

_____

_____

_____

_____

_____

_____

_____

_____

_____

_____

_____

_____

_____

_____

_____

Notes

· ·

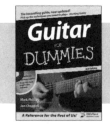

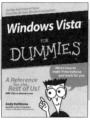

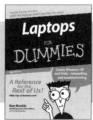

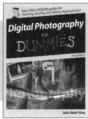

FOR

DUMMIES®

A Reference for the Rest of Us!

HISTORY

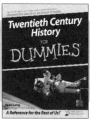

978-0-470-51015-5

978-0-470-03536-8

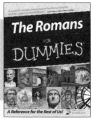

978-0-470-03077-6

SPORT

978-0-470-01811-8

978-0-470-03454-5

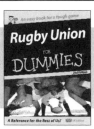

978-0-470-03537-5

LANGUAGES

978-0-7645-5194-9

978-0-7645-5193-2

978-0-7645-5196-3

Available wherever books are sold.

FOR DUMMIES

A Reference for the Rest of Us!

BUSINESS & FINANCE

978-0-470-51648-5

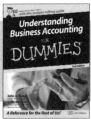

978-0-470-99245-6

978-0-470-99280-7

HOME & PROPERTY

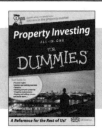

978-0-470-51502-0

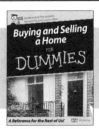

978-0-7645-7027-8

978-0-7645-7054-4

REFERENCE

978-0-470-05752-0

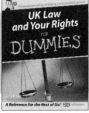

978-0-470-02796-7

978-0-470-06038-4

Available wherever books are sold.